HELLO HOLY SPIRIT

God's Gift of Live-in Help

Dianne Leman

Hello, Holy Spirit
God's Gift of Live-in Help

Published by: fox and hare publications

ISBN-13: 978-1543177350

Scriptures taken from:

The Message. Copyright © by Eugene H. Peterson 1993, 1994, 1995, 1996, 2000, 2001, 2002. Used by permission of NavPress Publishing Group.

NASB—NEW AMERICAN STANDARD BIBLE ®, Copyright © 1960,1962,1963,1968,1971,1 972,1973,1975,1977,1995 by The Lockman Foundation. Used by permission.

NLT—Holy Bible, New Living Translation, copyright 1996, 2004. Used by permission of Tyndale House Publishers, Wheaton, Illinois 60189. All rights reserved.

ESV—English Standard Version copyright 2001 by Crossway, a publishing ministry of Good News publishers. Used by permission. All rights reserved.

NKJV— The New King James Version. Copyright © 1979, 1980, 1982, Thomas Nelson Publishers, Inc.

Cover Design: Katie Goulet
Interior Design: Jody Boles

http://www.dianneleman.com/

fox and hare publications

Dedication

To all who are thirsty...

The Spirit and the Bride say, "Come."
And let the one who hears say, "Come."
And let the one who is thirsty come;
let the one who wishes take the water of life
without cost (Revelation 22:17).

Table of Contents

Introduction: The Gift That Changes Everything

"Hello, Holy Spirit!" Now, that's an unusual greeting. Do I usually go around talking to spirits? Do I often say hello to ghosts? Let me assure you, no, I do not. You see, the Holy Spirit is NOT a ghost or a force or an impersonal power. He is a Person. As a matter of fact, the Holy Spirit is God. And He is God's gift to each of us. He is given to help us with our lives, our everyday lives, in every way.

 I love to wake up each morning and say, "Hello, Holy Spirit. I welcome Your help today." He is always ready and willing to provide me with all the help I need to live a joyful life of purpose and peace. This makes getting out of bed so much easier!

Desperate for Help

But it was not always this way with me. Oh, I knew I needed help. As a matter of fact, I was desperate for help. I was a hard-working college graduate, adept at solving most of life's problems with my own knowledge, money, or other human resources. However, at 24 years old, I encountered a problem that all the help from medicine, money, and man could not solve. I had exhausted the best that these options offered. I was told by medical and religious experts alike that I would most likely never conceive the child my husband and I so desperately wanted. I was desperate for my dead, barren womb to carry a child. I was frustrated with the inability of my dead, barren faith to help me. I needed help, real help. Not tiring self-help. Not more expensive medical help. Not trite religious help. Not halfway help. I needed real, life-altering *help*. God knew this. God loved me. And God had real help for me.

> Even though I was a churchgoing, water-baptized believer in Jesus, I had never known or experienced the Holy Spirit. If anything, I had only heard vague warnings to be careful of "crazy charismatics."

The Spirit Moves

It was the '70s, 1977 to be exact, and God's Spirit was sweeping across the land and around the globe. He surprised thousands of people with His life-changing power and presence. History would later label this the Charismatic Movement as it swelled into several decades of impact on individuals, churches, and denominations all over the world. I was one of those impacted individuals. Even though I was a churchgoing, water-baptized believer in Jesus, I had never known or experienced the Holy Spirit. If anything, I had only heard vague warnings to be careful of "crazy charismatics." My mature mentors in the faith told me that such folks were "deceived and too emotional." And those voices were joined by the scoffs of my peers: "Those 'Spirit nuts' are just plain weird!"

Crazy, deceived, emotional, weird… was this Holy Spirit dangerous? I had no idea, but I needed help—help that no one and no thing had provided. "Help, God!" I cried.

God loves to answer that cry of "Help!" He knows that our needs make us vulnerable (in a good way) to His "craziness"—to His crazy charisma and His powerful grace and gifts. He wants to impact us with a gift that changes everything—a gift of "live-in" help—His very own Holy Spirit. And, yes, the Holy Spirit is the ultimate "crazy charismatic."

Total Life Change

Meeting the Holy Spirit radically changed—and is still changing—my life from the inside out. Not only did I get filled to overflowing with the Holy Spirit and receive a miraculous healing for my barren womb ("overflowing" with five children and now 16 grands), but I have also witnessed and shared in the Holy Spirit's transformation of thousands of other people in my unexpected life as a pastor. The Holy Spirit is truly God's gift that changes everything. He brings a total life makeover.

God's Gift of Himself

This change affects the significant things in life: our identity and destiny, our happiness and heartaches, our health and hurts, our faith and fear. The Holy Spirit can also change the smaller, but no less important things in our life: our relationships, habits, work, finances, and leisure. He is a gift from God Himself. Actually, the gift *is* God Himself. He is live-in help because God moves inside of us. We are His home. Crazy, I know! That's what I thought. Now, 40 years later, I know I can't (and won't ever) do life without Him. Why would I? He changes everything for the absolute best. My heart sings, "I love You, Holy Spirit! You are God's gracious gift—given freely to all Your beloved children. You make life crazy good!"

God is Eager

God is so eager to lavish His love and His Spirit on everyone. He has something far better than self-help. Thank God! He gives us live-in help—Spirit help. He knows our needs better than we do. He knows our fears and our failures. He knows our successes and our stupidity. He knows our passions and our pains, our deepest disappointments and our wildest dreams. He loves us so much and wants to give us the power to do what we cannot do on our own. He knows we need help. Jesus says:

> *I will ask the Father, and He will give you another Helper (the Holy Spirit), that He may be with you forever (John 14:16 NASB).*

> The Father gives us the Helper and He never leaves us, no matter what. That is amazing. Even if we mess up, He does not bolt. Why would He? He is given to help us, and when we blow it, we need help the most.

The Father gives us the Helper and He never leaves us, no matter what. That is amazing. Even if we mess up, He does not bolt. Why would He? He is given to help us, and when we blow it, we need help the most.

He wants us to experience His powerful help in all ways—whether reading the Bible or reading a novel; worshipping Jesus or walking in the woods; praying to the Father or playing baseball; serving the poor or serving dinner to the family; attending church or attending a movie; prophesying to a stranger or putting our children to bed; raising wheat or raising the dead. Yep! The Holy Spirit is God's gift of live-in help for *all* of life.

Help Needed, Help Wanted

So, I ask you, "How's it going for you? Are you happy with your life? Are you satisfied with your relationships, your health, your work, your finances, and your foreseeable future? Is your faith in God resulting in joy, peace, and power in all of life?" If so, then this book will be a refresher for what you already know. If, on the other hand, there is an ache inside you—perhaps regret over the past, fear of the future, or confusion about anything in life— keep reading, because your help is literally very near.

Most people need and want help with their everyday lives. They want help with their work, family, health, finances, habits, leisure, and yes, their whole lives, including their faith. Many access self-help resources, counselors, life coaches, seminars, retreats, conferences, and treatments galore, as Google and Facebook readily testify. Much of this can be helpful. But many people are unaware, skeptical, or even downright scared of the amazing help God has readily supplied.

Wake-up Call

God never intended for us to handle life alone. He never meant to leave us to our own devices, strength, know-how, and abilities. I mean, really… how miserable is that? Sometimes, it takes us awhile to admit our need, but eventually most of us wake up and realize we need help. We're often not sure where or how to receive that help. We've already looked in many places (some dangerous) and to many things (some not so good) for that perfect solution. Broke and broken, we discover once again, we need help. We are not satisfied.

Created to Live in Union

Of course we are not satisfied. We are unique creations, designed in the image of God Himself and made to live in happy union with God our Father, Jesus the Son, and the Holy Spirit—our Helper. God wants to empower us to live in this full and satisfying union—whether we are fighting a war, a cold, or a spouse. He wants to flood us with happiness at the pool, the parent conference, or the party. He made us for happy union with Him at all times, in all places.

Not So Much

Happy union with God? Not so much. This certainly wasn't the picture I had of the so-called Christian life. The Christian life I saw modeled was harnessed with thousands of rules and regulations: no movies, no sports, no concerts, no TV, no dancing, no dating, no fun! The church I knew seemed more intent on creating "Christian Clones"—members who looked alike, thought alike, acted alike, but pretty much did not *like* anything to do with real life! I had no idea that life with God might include a twirl across the ballroom floor or the delight of seeing *The Lion King* on Broadway. I had no idea the God of the universe offered me a life of intimacy and enjoyment with Him, whether I was in the pew or in the park. The Holy Spirit would convince me otherwise.

Controversies and Questions

The Holy Spirit has truly been a controversial subject for a long time, even though the Bible and people's lives are filled with clear evidence of His character and work. While the Holy Spirit has become a more popular subject in recent years, there are still many people who've never heard of Him and even more who've never actually experienced Him. There are others who have some pretty mixed up theology about Him. Some may have all the correct theology about this third Person of the Trinity, but they lack any real relationship with Him. Many reject His powerful presence, point fingers at those who welcome Him, and accuse them of being "deceived," "too emotional," or "one of those crazy charismatics." Others are genuinely skeptical, cynical, or just plain ignorant about the Holy Spirit.

But, the Holy Spirit is no wimpy wind! He is God and He blows—how, when, and where He wills. We have a choice. We can turn our faces and enjoy that Wind or we can run to escape the Whirlwind! But, we will never put the Wind in a box. Go ahead, try!

Yes, for centuries, people have tried to control the Spirit. Why do people resist the Spirit? Why do some seek to diminish His gifts (e.g., healing, miracles, tongues, prophecy), and focus only on His fruit (e.g., joy, self-control, patience, and kindness)? Why do so many say they are "Spirit-filled," and yet there is no River of Life flowing out of their innermost beings? Why do people strive so hard to "be holy" when the Holy Spirit longs to impart His holiness to us?

Answers

Thankfully, the Holy Spirit Himself answers these questions and controversies. We look to Him for understanding in this book. We know He brings clarity and focus to Jesus's statement about our new life—available after Jesus rose from the dead:

> *In that day you will know that I am in My Father, and you in Me, and I in you (John 14:20 ESV).*

God lives in us; we live in God. This is not normal or natural to most of us. We have much to learn. Yes, we are designed to live in vital union with God the Father, Son, and Spirit. The Holy Spirit Himself reveals and empowers that very life in us. He is God's gift of live-in help. We are God's home, His temple, and the Spirit is our Helper. The supernatural gifts are His, given to us to help in ministry and life. The fruits are His, too, the harvest of a life lived in union with Him.

God's Empowering Presence

We love a Trinitarian God—Father, Son, and Holy Spirit—three Persons, one God. This coequal, coeternal Trinity, while a mystery in many ways, is so critical to our full experience of the life God designed for His beloved sons and daughters. We live with God's very own Empowering Presence, the Holy Spirit, within us. The Holy Spirit can be known personally as a Teacher of Truth and experienced powerfully as a Ministry Partner. He can also be deeply loved as a Best Friend, Joyful Companion, and Constant Comforter. But the Holy Spirit is no cosmic "errand boy." He is God, and His residence inside of us assures us that God is always with us, helping us at all times and in all ways for the best.

> The Spirit makes it possible for us to live in delightful union with the Father, Son, and Himself. This is the same relational union that our God has enjoyed from all eternity. He wants His children to enjoy this oneness with Him. He wants us to know our true identities as adopted, loved, righteous sons and daughters.

Revelation of Union

The Spirit's love transforms our lives—from the inside out. He makes it possible for us to overflow with righteousness, peace, joy, and power. This is the life that God intended for all His children. Rather than "overshadowing Jesus" as some may fear, the Holy Spirit (who is called the Spirit of Christ in Romans 8:9) reveals more and more of Jesus and brings intimacy with Him. The Spirit makes it possible for us to live in delightful union with the Father, Son, and Himself. This is the same relational union that our God has enjoyed from all eternity. He wants His children to enjoy this oneness with Him. He wants us to know our true identities as adopted, loved, righteous sons and daughters. He even trusts us and sends us to continue the ministry of Jesus here on earth: announcing the Kingdom, healing the sick, and raising the dead. Such a life is impossible without the Holy Spirit, God's Empowering Presence.

"Hello, Holy Spirit!"

This book is written to give every person an easy-to-understand theology and simple, practical steps for embracing the Holy Spirit as God's gift of live-in help. We desire for each reader to have the joy of saying with ease, "Hello, Holy Spirit!" We want all to experience the life-changing help of the Spirit every day.

Each chapter answers a question and then explores how the Holy Spirit is God's gift that changes everything:

- Chapter One: Help! Who Are You, Holy Spirit?
- Chapter Two: Help! What Do You Do, Holy Spirit?
- Chapter Three: Help! How Do I Encounter You, Holy Spirit?
- Chapter Four: Help! How Do I Experience You Daily, Holy Spirit?
- Chapter Five: Help! How Do I Trust You in Tough Times, Holy Spirit?
- Chapter Six: Help! How Do I Pray for Others, Holy Spirit?

At the end of each chapter there are questions for you to reflect on and respond to. Take some time to think and pray. Join with a small group to discuss your thoughts. Together, view the accompanying DVD of short teachings and stories told by ordinary people about their experiences with the Holy Spirit. Learn, laugh, cry together, and watch the Holy Spirit change your life. Access some of the resources listed. This is a journey, and transformation does not occur overnight or alone. But the Holy Spirit is the gift that changes everything—for the absolute best.

Life-changing Encounters

There are usually just a few experiences in our lives that end up radically shifting who we are and where we are going. It may be a chance, unexpected meeting with the person who becomes our loving spouse. It might be a tragic event that, while painful, turned us in an unforeseen and positive direction we would not have otherwise gone. It may have been a book randomly picked up at an out-of-the-way bookstore whose contents altered all we believed for eternity.

For me, one of these life-changing experiences was meeting the Holy Spirit. I had no idea who He was. I was not actively seeking Him. Little did I know at that time in the spring of 1977 how this encounter would change my life completely. Now, 40 years later, I am overwhelmed with such thankfulness for all He is in me and through me.

My Prayer

My prayer is that those who read this book will experience a radical encounter with God's gift of live-in help, His Holy Spirit, who alone can change everything, now and forever. My desire is that thousands more will awaken each morning to say: "Hello, Holy Spirit!" and will enjoy His presence and power in all they do.

For many years, I prayed these inspired words written by Paul, and I pray them today for all who read this book:

> *When I think of the wisdom and scope of His plan, I fall down on my knees and pray to the Father of all the great family of God—some of them already in heaven and some down here on earth— that out of His glorious, unlimited resources He will give you the mighty inner strengthening of* **His Holy Spirit.** *And I pray that* **Christ will be more and more at home in your hearts,** *living within you as you trust in Him.*
>
> *May your roots go down deep into the soil of God's marvelous love; and may you be able to feel and understand, as all God's children should, how long, how wide, how deep, and how high His love really is; and to experience this love for yourselves, though it is so great that you will never see the end of it or fully know or understand it. And so at last you will be filled up with God Himself.*
>
> *Now glory be to God, who by His mighty power at work within us is able to do far more than we would ever dare to ask or even dream of— infinitely beyond our highest prayers, desires, thoughts, or hopes. May He be given glory forever and ever through endless ages because of His master plan of salvation for the Church through Jesus Christ (Ephesians 3:14-21 TLB; emphasis mine).*

Welcome, Holy Spirit!
Dianne Leman
February 2017

Chapter One:
Help! Who Are You, Holy Spirit?

The Holy Spirit is God, the third Person of the Trinity. He is eager to reveal Himself and be in relationship with everyone as "the Helper." He woos us, reveals God to us, and offers us a new birth, complete with a heart transplant. Get ready for a new friend and a new life.

Life on the campus of a Big Ten university was intoxicating—in more ways than one. Raised in a strict, religious family, I was your typical good girl in high school who suddenly found herself footloose and fancy free, a hundred miles from home. I was quickly immersed in the liberal and liberated lifestyle of challenging ideas and thoughts. I loved learning and soon discarded the simplistic, unsophisticated, and stifling beliefs of my family's faith. In addition, I plunged headlong into the world of an exclusive Greek sorority, complete with parties, bar nights, and friendships with people very different from myself. It was both exhilarating and frightening at the same time.

I was free! God was far away—if He even existed—and I was on the run. Just in case He was for real, I was determined that this "Policeman in the Sky"—the God I had been raised to fear—would never catch me.

The Holy Spirit Woos

Ah, but I had no clue how much this God loved me and how determined He was to gently woo me by His Spirit. Despite my 18 years in the church, I had never really heard of the Holy Spirit. I had endured countless hours listening to boring Bible teachers who flat-out ignored Him. But, thankfully, the Holy Spirit knew me and longed to reveal to me how much the Father loved me, Dianne Marie. He wanted me to know how amazing Jesus is and what a gift He, the Holy Spirit, is to me. Such profound revelation is for you, too, because God does not play favorites.

> Like a wise, yet winsome lover, the Holy Spirit woos. Unlike humans, the Spirit is not easily thwarted by rejection. He is quite adept at pursuing us, even when we resist Him, ignore Him, or even grieve Him.

The Holy Spirit desires to do this for every human being. Like a wise, yet winsome lover, the Holy Spirit woos. Unlike humans, the Spirit is not easily thwarted by rejection. He is quite adept at pursuing us, even when we resist Him, ignore Him, or even grieve Him. He gently, persistently, lovingly woos us. He is a determined Lover. I say, "Watch out—He is good at it and He won't stop, ever. Thank God!"

He is a Person

So, who is this Holy Spirit? He is not a ghost, an impersonal force, or an elusive power "out there." He is neither a doctrine to be studied nor a Distant Deity to be feared. He is a Person to be known and loved. He is God Himself. He is one of three Persons of the Trinity—Father, Son, and Holy Spirit—one God, three Persons. He is God's gift of Himself to each of us. He makes the Christian life indescribably beautiful and a fun-filled delight. Go figure! Who knew that being a Christian could be so much fun?

He Reveals God

For starters, the Holy Spirit makes sure we really know God. Some of us have pretty mixed-up ideas about God, and these make it difficult to enjoy life. We may see God as a tormenting Grinch or an unconcerned Deity or a jolly, indulgent Santa Claus—all twisted images of God. And, if we have had an earthly father who was abusive, absent, or just plain dysfunctional, then our image of Father God is distorted and we are damaged. But not beyond repair.

We also have confused ideas about Jesus. Many of these are perpetrated by woeful paintings of Him: white-faced and weak, holding a lamb, or else bloodied and beaten, hanging on a cross. The Holy Spirit loves to show us the real Jesus—the powerful, passionate, and personal Jesus. For some of us, He first reveals that God is "more than a word." He is a God who loves and cares for us—way before we even know it.

God Becomes "More Than a Word"

"I was driving 100 miles per hour, going over a dangerous country hill with a carload of my best friends, when we hit an oncoming truck full force. We should have all been dead," said a sober 35-year-old man named Stephen. "But, to the shock of the police and the EMTs, we all escaped without serious injury. This was the first time I knew that God was more than a word. He was real, for sure! I should have been a goner."

When did God became "more than a word" to you? This is always a work of the Spirit, sometimes incognito (or not, as in the case of Stephen!), and it is often your first experience with the Holy Spirit—although you might be unaware at the time. You may not have believed in God or really known Him, but you experienced something (or Someone) that opened your eyes to a different reality. Maybe you survived a similar car accident or "co-incidentally" ended up in the right place at the right time for an amazing job or were delivered from an "impossible" jam. Suddenly, you knew God was definitely "more than a word." He was real, and He had somehow touched your life. This doesn't mean you necessarily did anything about it at the time. It just means that the Holy Spirit was showing you God in a way you never knew before—a God who heard your cry, loved you, or was looking out for you. You may have met Him later... or are about to meet Him now!

God Knows We Need Help

Satan and sin brought, and continue to bring, so much destruction and devastation into the world. Relationships miserably fail; bodies are ravaged with disease; tragic accidents take lives. Poverty, violence, and a host of horrific outcomes wreak havoc in individuals, nations, and throughout all of history. Hearts grow stony, stubborn, and selfish. God's beloved creation needs help.

Help Comes!

The Holy Spirit visits a virgin named Mary and she gives birth to a Son, Jesus, who is fully God and fully man. This same Holy Spirit empowers Jesus to announce and demonstrate a brand new day and way of life, called the Kingdom of God. Here, sinful renegades are transformed into new people, blind people receive their sight, deaf people hear, the poor are fed, and even the dead are raised back to life. But sin and sinful people, under the rule of Satan, crucify this God-Man, Jesus, on a cross, and seal Him in a rock-hewn tomb. Just three days later, the Holy Spirit resurrects Jesus, because Jesus is totally free of sin, and death cannot hold him. Jesus is the firstborn from the dead and now offers new life to all. New birth becomes available for every human being.

Life Interrupted

It was a crisp September afternoon, 1971. Class was over for the day. Spaghetti was simmering on the stove. It was just a few moments before my hubby of one month would come bounding in the door, hungry for dinner. I plopped down on the comfy, secondhand sofa in our rental house at 405 N. Mathews on the campus of the University of Illinois. I was eager to continue reading *Christy*, a book someone had given me. Reading was my favorite pastime, but a heavy school load limited my free time. Hence, this was a rare, precious moment. I do not recall knowing *Christy* was a Christian book. Since I was not a believer and had no interest in becoming one, I would not have selected it. It was a gift from a friend who knew I loved to read and knew I loved teaching, like the book's main character. Unknown to me, the Holy Spirit was about to use this book to interrupt my life, thrusting me into a dramatically different direction.

"I Want to Know Jesus"

The novel, *Christy*, written by Catherine Marshall, is a historical fiction story inspired by Catherine's own mother. As a young woman, Christy went to teach impoverished Appalachian children, and the book details her experiences of faith, mountain life, and learning. One character in the book, a Quaker woman named Alice, captured my attention. Her faith was vibrant, alive, and personal—unlike anything I had ever witnessed or experienced growing up in a strict, religious home. As a matter of fact, both my husband and I had agreed we were absolutely not interested in ever becoming Christians, joining a church, or having anything at all to do with faith. While we loved and honored our godly parents, we knew such a life was not for us. So, you can imagine my utter surprise when, as I am quietly reading this novel, tears begin to stream down my face, seemingly out of nowhere. Then, I heard these words coming out of my mouth, "I want to know Jesus, just like Alice."

Yes, I want to know Jesus. Even though I was raised in a godly Christian home, taken to church every week, and heard the Bible taught, I certainly did not know Jesus, at least not the Jesus that I was reading about in *Christy*. This was a Jesus who was warm, loving, personal, kind. This was a Jesus who was intimately involved in a woman's day-to-day life. This was a Jesus who could be known and loved. Little did I know that such a prompting, such a divine invitation coming from the innermost part of my being, was actually the Holy Spirit. He was drawing me to saving faith in Jesus. He was giving me the desire to know Jesus. He was invading my life. I was about to be born anew.

Born Anew!

I was about to become the new being Jesus designed me to be all along. I was about to enter into the most exhilarating relationship of a lifetime. The old Dianne was about to die and rise again with a brand new heart, a new spirit, and the Spirit of Jesus Himself living in me. This was God's promise written many years before by the Prophet Ezekiel:

> *And I will give you a new heart, and I will put a new spirit in you. I will take out your stony, stubborn heart and give you a tender, responsive heart. And I will put my Spirit in you... (Ezekiel 36:26-27 NLT).*

Of course, I had no idea what was happening. This was all a mystery to me. I thought I had to clean up my life and make myself good enough for God before He would even think about accepting me, let alone allow me to know Him.

> Jesus did all the hard work for me to be born again. His death and resurrection made it possible for me to be born again. This seemed too easy, too good to be true. ·Did I believe?

This new birth is a mystery and a miracle. Just as a human birth is a miracle with the mama doing all the hard work of pushing the baby through the birth canal, Jesus did all the hard work for me to be born again. His death and resurrection made it possible for me to be born again. This seemed too easy, too good to be true. Did I believe?

Believe

You do have to respond to the Holy Spirit's nudge. You do have to believe. But all you need is childlike faith. Just a simple, "Yes, Jesus, I want to know you." He does the hard part of miraculously making us a new creation. He replaces our old, stony, stubborn hearts with new, tender, responsive hearts. He puts His very own Spirit in us. That is just the beginning, as it is with the birth of any baby. There are many years of growth ahead.

For over 45 years, I have never stopped saying, "Jesus, I want to know you more." And the Spirit has never disappointed me. He helps me know Jesus more intimately every day. He shows me how to live as a new creation. I am still learning.

Agent of the New Birth

The Holy Spirit is the agent of this new birth. He is the one who draws us, changes us, and works in us the amazing reality of being made new, clean, and now the actual home of God Himself. This is all possible because of Jesus's work on the cross and His powerful resurrection. Jesus welcomes us into God's reign and rule—the Kingdom of God. We now have eternal life, the "God-kind" of life. And that Kingdom—that life—is IN us! Jesus tells us:

For indeed, the Kingdom of God is within you (Luke 17:21b NKJV).

The Spirit cries out in us, "I want to know Jesus." He stirs faith in our hearts so we can believe and trust this Jesus. While it is all somewhat mysterious and definitely out of our total control, the Holy Spirit's work in bringing us new life is powerful and unmistakable. He brings us this miraculous birth from above, a birth by the Spirit Himself. Jesus explained the mystery in this way:

Jesus answered, "Truly, truly, I say to you, unless one is born of water and the Spirit he cannot enter into the Kingdom of God. That which is born of the flesh is flesh, and that which is born of the Spirit is spirit. Do not be amazed that I said to you, 'You must be born again.' The wind blows where it wishes and you hear the sound of it, but do not know where it comes from and where it is going; so is everyone who is born of the Spirit" (John 3:5-8 NLT).

Yes, the new birth, engineered by the Holy Spirit, is often like the wind whose effects we see, hear, and feel, but whose origin and actual presence and direction we cannot discern. Nevertheless, we can choose to believe and receive this amazing truth of being born anew by God's Spirit and ushered into the Kingdom of God AND have the Kingdom ushered into us!

An Imperfect Illustration

An imperfect illustration may help you to grasp this miracle: when a baby girl is born, she already has within her every egg that could possibly one day unite with a sperm to create a new life. In the same way, every human being carries the "egg" of God's image, even though most of us do a pretty good job of obscuring that image through sin. Yet, when by the "wind" of the Spirit we hear the Good News of Jesus offering us new birth, the "sperm" of faith unites with the "egg" of His image in us and a new life is conceived! We are "born of the Spirit." A new creation is birthed, thanks to the Holy Spirit.

I am so convinced of the Holy Spirit's ability and desire to reveal Himself to each person, according to each one's need, history, and personality, I will defer to Him. If you do not yet have this new heart, I believe that He is already tugging on you. He is already gently nudging you to lay down your defenses and relinquish your big "buts." You can trust Him. He loves to reveal Himself to each one of us. He is a genius at showing us Jesus and the Father—One God, three Persons. Just believe.

Not in a Hurry

The Holy Spirit is never in a hurry. He patiently and gently woos us into relationship with our loving Father. He wants to show us that our Father sees us as His beloved, valuable sons and daughters, made in His image, restored to original innocence by Jesus, and given a new birth. He sees each one of us with a rich destiny to be enjoyed, regardless of one's stupid mistakes, sinful past, and damaged history. He trusts the Holy Spirit to continue His powerful work of making this known to each of us, bringing us new birth in Jesus.

Each Birth is Unique

Every Christian has his or her unique story of being born again. Many know the exact time and place. For others, it was a more gradual process, or it happened when they were very young, so the details are less precise or memorable. Nevertheless, every experience is valid if it results in each person realizing he or she is a new creation in Jesus.

Interestingly, Jesus never had anyone pray what the church commonly calls "the sinner's prayer," where one specifically acknowledges his sinfulness and sorrow and confesses faith in Jesus as the Savior. As a pastor for over 40 years, I have used the sinner's prayer many times with people who are coming into relationship with Jesus for the first time. It is a helpful tool. However, I am more convinced than ever that the Holy Spirit knows best how to draw each unique person to Jesus, and a person does not necessarily have to repeat a specific set of words or prayer.

I always want to stay sensitive to the Spirit when talking and praying with people who do not yet know Jesus. There is no magic bullet in getting people to "pray the prayer." It may even be dangerous in that it somehow inoculates people against a real invasion of God's saving Presence, the Holy Spirit, because they think they prayed to become a Christian, but they really had no faith or were forced. They prayed or repeated a prayer under duress or in doubt, opening their mouths to let words spill out without opening their hearts to let Jesus enter in. Not surprisingly, their lives do not change. They were not hungry to grow—unlike all newborn babies, who are voracious eaters. No, just repeating some words does not necessarily bring about the new birth.

The New Birth is Miraculous

The new birth that the Holy Spirit unveils is truly a miracle birth. We cry: "I once was lost and now I am found. I once was blind and now I see. I once was foolish and disobedient, full of all kinds of evil, and now I am new, righteous, and full of the Holy Spirit." This is the amazing Good News of the entire Bible made possible through Jesus Christ our Savior. Here is how Paul the apostle described it:

> *Once we, too, were foolish and disobedient. We were misled and became slaves to many lusts and pleasures. Our lives were full of evil and envy, and we hated each other.*
>
> *But—When God our Savior revealed His kindness and love, He saved us, not because of the righteous things we had done, but because of His mercy. He washed away our sins, giving us a NEW BIRTH AND NEW LIFE through the HOLY SPIRIT. He generously poured out the SPIRIT upon us through Jesus Christ our Savior.*
>
> *Because of His grace He declared us righteous and gave us confidence that we will inherit eternal life (Titus 3:3-7 NLT; emphasis mine).*

We have new life through the Holy Spirit. Our sins are gone. We have a generous dose of the Spirit, who empowers us to live this new life. What is this new life like? I'm glad you asked, because this is another important aspect of who the Holy Spirit is.

He Wants Us to Know Who We Are

He not only wants us to know who He (God) is, but He is also determined that we know who *we* are. When we know who we are, we can live a full and satisfying life, the eternal life He gives us now. A key phrase in the Titus text is "Because of His grace, He declared us righteous." What does that mean? Sounds kind of religious to me. Hold on. This is a very important description of what occurred in the new birth. Understanding this will make a huge difference in your life as a disciple of Jesus.

I must admit that for many years, I did not have the full revelation of God's grace and His declaration that I am righteous. (And I am still learning.) But this revelation of God's grace and Jesus's gift of righteousness for us is something the Spirit is specifically pouring out now in the 21st century (although it is centuries old!). God wants us to know our identity as His loved, righteous sons and daughters, fully clean and holy now.

Our Righteousness is a Gift

Christianity is vastly different from all other religions in that it is the only faith where righteousness—made right in relationship with God and right in being—is a total gift from our God. There is nothing we can or have to do to earn being right with God. There is no work we can or have to do to keep it. As the Scripture in Titus says, it is not because of anything righteous we have done that causes our loving, merciful, and kind God to save us. No, it is all His grace—His unmerited, divine favor and influence that is given to us completely free, no strings attached. These are Paul's words:

We are made right with God by placing our faith in Jesus Christ. And this is true for everyone who believes, no matter who we are. For everyone has sinned; we all fall short of God's glorious standard. Yet God, with undeserved kindness (grace), declares that we are righteous. He did this through Christ Jesus when He freed us from the penalty for our sins (Romans 3:22-24 NLT).

Jesus is Our Righteousness. Jesus makes us right with God, now and forever. This gift of righteousness assures us of total acceptance as sons and daughters of God and gives us the privilege of having an intimate relationship with our Father. This brings freedom and joy to being a Christian.

We are made right by faith in Jesus—by trusting Him. And even this faith is a gift from God, released by the Holy Spirit. This is true for everybody, no matter how bad or how good. We are declared righteous by grace—not by our deserving it through our "good works"—because Jesus freed us from sin and its penalty. Jesus is our Righteousness. Jesus makes us right with God, now and forever. This gift of righteousness assures us of total acceptance as sons and daughters of God and gives us the privilege of having an intimate relationship with our Father. This brings freedom and joy to being a Christian.

This is unheard of in any other major world religion. We get to be in an actual, intimate, loving relationship with God, who declares us righteous in our being and in His sight. This is not an imputed righteousness where God just looks at us differently because of Jesus's work. That would be fake righteousness! No, this is real righteousness. We have a redeemed innocence. And this makes intimacy with God possible and real.

Shame and Condemnation Gone!

I did not always know this. I lived with much shame and condemnation. Yes, I knew my relationship with God was restored and I was saved and going to heaven someday, but I did not comprehend the incredible gift of being made right, not only in standing with God, but also in my inner being. Now I know I am righteous and I have no more shame and no more condemnation. All my sins are gone—past, present, future—thanks to the miraculous work of Jesus.

Do I always feel like it? No. Do I always act like it? No. But, because I know this is a precious gift, bought with the blood of Jesus, I am so motivated to live right. And Jesus lives in me by His Spirit to ensure that I have the power to walk in righteousness.

Jesus is Our Righteousness

Jesus Himself personally and perfectly obeyed the Law and fulfilled all righteousness for us. He did what we could not do. Then He went to the Cross, paid the penalty of death and shed blood for our sin, defeated our enemy, Satan, and rose again, offering us the free gift of His righteousness. This is Good News!

> *For our sake He made Him (Jesus) to be sin who knew no sin, so that in Him we might become the righteousness of God (2 Corinthians 5:21 ESV).*

Faith in Him now and every day eradicates shame, empowers us to live righteously, and enables us to enjoy being free as sons and daughters of the Living God. The righteous live by faith. How do we do this? By believing in Him and what He has done. By welcoming Jesus to live in us by His Spirit. By knowing we are righteous and then choosing to live with the Presence of the Holy Spirit empowering us. This is simple faith in the One who died for each one of us, took us with Him into the grave, and rose victorious over sin, death, and Satan.

The Holy Spirit Reveals Jesus's Victory is Our Victory

The Holy Spirit is so good at revealing to us the deep significance of Jesus and His victory on the Cross. But the Holy Spirit is also determined that we know and experience another very important truth for living out this new birth. Just as important for my life and yours is the fact that another death occurred on Jesus's cross.

Did you know we died on that cross with Jesus? Did you know we were buried with Him in the grave? Paul writes:

> *I have been crucified with Christ. It is no longer I who live, but Christ who lives in me. And the life I now live in the flesh I live by faith in the Son of God, who loved me and gave Himself for me. I do not nullify the grace of God, for if righteousness were through the law, then Christ died for no purpose (Galatians 2:20-21 ESV).*

This sounds somewhat mysterious, but it is totally true. The old, sinful, unholy, shame-filled Dianne died with Jesus Christ on that cross. Then, in Christ, I was raised up and born again by the Holy Spirit. Christ now lives in me. The life I live every day in the flesh, here and now, I live by the faith of Jesus and by faith *in* Jesus, who loves me and gave His life for me.

Jesus's victory is my victory. I will not nullify or make the grace of God ineffective by trying to earn, work for, get good enough, or make myself right and righteous in His sight. No, that was the whole purpose of Jesus's death on the cross. I simply believe what He has done for me and I receive His righteousness and His Spirit to live in me. I have a new life and a new heart in Jesus. I believe this.

You Mean My Heart is Not Wicked?

For too many years in my life as a Christian, I had the mistaken belief that my new heart was somehow still wicked. I had been taught (and sadly, even taught this myself) that the heart is sick and we have to work hard to bring health to our new heart:

> *The heart is more deceitful than all else and is desperately sick; Who can understand it? (Jeremiah 17:9).*

That is our old heart. This is why Jesus had to die for us. We have a new heart now—thanks to Jesus! But I thought even my new heart was still sick and wicked. This belief resulted in behavior and practices that I thought would make my "wicked" heart better. I prayed, read the Bible, fasted, served others, and undertook other practices to help "doctor" my sick heart. I received inner healing prayer to uproot all the wickedness inside me.

Now, I am not saying these practices are wrong. But, I engaged in them to fix myself. I relied on *my work* and not on *Jesus's work.* Jesus made it possible for me to have a totally new heart. Why would I nullify the grace of God in trying to fix the old me? Jesus paid an enormous price to make me a new creation:

> *Therefore, if anyone is in Christ, he is a new creation. The old has passed away; behold, the new has come (2 Corinthians 5:17 ESV).*

The old, wicked heart is gone. We have received new, pure, healthy hearts. We are new creations. We are born anew. But, we may wonder, why do we still have old ways or habits or thoughts?

A Heart Transplant

I think we can gain some valuable insight by thinking about this in medical and physical terms for a moment and look at someone who literally received a new heart—through a heart transplant.

Peter, from London, England, faced imminent death due to a badly diseased heart. His only hope was a heart transplant. As a last resort, he got on the transplant list. One day, Peter got the call telling him that 23-year-old Colin had died in a car accident. Within hours, Peter had received a new heart from Colin. Of course, Peter was so thankful to his donor. Peter met Colin's mother and expressed his deep indebtedness to her for the donation of Colin's heart. Peter had a new healthy heart, thanks to Colin. He was a new man.

Did Peter just go back to life as usual? No! With a new heart, he had to learn a whole new way of life, or he could seriously damage the new heart. It would be senseless and tragic for Peter to throw away such a precious gift by not caring properly for it. What a slap in the face it would be to Colin's mother if Peter abused his new heart. Peter adopted a new way of life to care for his new heart—eating, exercising, living, and loving in healthier ways than before. He was a changed man. He so adapted to his new heart and new way of life that he ran the London Marathon. Colin's mother was even there, cheering him on! It was her victory, too.

Parallels

There are so many parallels to our receiving new hearts from Jesus. When we receive our new hearts, it is only possible because Someone has died. Someone dies so another can live. Yes, Jesus is that Someone who died so we may live. Peter (and any recipient) who needs a new heart can do nothing to deserve a new heart. Jesus is the ultimate organ donor. He gave His whole life that we might have brand new hearts. There is nothing we could do to deserve this. Our old hearts were diseased, and we were dead in sin.

We trusted Jesus, received new hearts, and our lives now reflect this life change. First and foremost, we overflow with thankfulness to our Donor, Jesus. We have a heartfelt determination to live differently—for Him. We want to be victorious in this marathon called life. If we wanted to run an actual marathon, we would need to make big changes in our lives to run a successful race. Will we make big changes in our lives for Jesus?

Our Challenge

Here is our challenge. We need to learn how to live with our new hearts from Jesus. This takes time. Since our minds and bodies are not new, we have to learn new ways of living with new hearts from Jesus.

When a transplant patient receives a new heart, he cannot retain any of the old heart. That would be fatal. The old, diseased heart has to be surgically removed. In the same way, none of our old hearts—our old, sinful natures—remains. We have been crucified with Christ. We have been buried with Christ. We have risen with Christ and have brand new hearts, new lives, new natures, a new Spirit.

We do not have two hearts—a diseased, sinful heart and a new, clean one. However, we do need to do life differently in response to this gift of a new heart. We need a new lifestyle. Because it is not automatic, we have to learn new habits. A person who has major surgery to receive a new heart does not jump up and run a marathon. She learns a whole new way of life with this new heart. She learns to eat and drink differently. She learns to regularly exercise. She learns to properly rest, take her meds, and reduce stress. She still has the same mind and the same body. Old habits are there. She may even be tempted to live unwisely or go back to old ways, but that is dangerous.

In a similar way, do we just sin so grace can abound? No! We have new hearts. When we struggle, does that mean we still have old hearts? No! We are learning to live with new hearts, and that can be a challenge. Thankfully, we have the Helper, the Holy Spirit.

We Are Not Left to Ourselves

Although we are saved by grace and receive these amazing new hearts, some think (and act) as though now we have lots of work to do. They think that now it depends on self-effort, striving, and performing to successfully live the Christian life, overcome sin, and stay on the straight and narrow. No again!

> We are not left to ourselves. We have new hearts. And we each have our own personal trainer—the Holy Spirit. God's promise says: **I will put my Spirit in you!** How brilliant. We have our own personal trainer—One who lives IN us, empowers us, and strengthens us. We choose to interact with and depend on Him. This is not about willpower. This is about Spirit power.

We are not left to ourselves. We have new hearts. And we each have our own personal trainer—the Holy Spirit. God's promise says: **I will put my Spirit in you!** How brilliant. We have our own personal trainer—One who lives IN us, empowers us, and strengthens us. We choose to interact with and depend on Him. This is not about willpower. This is about Spirit power.

Training Requires Our Cooperation

Our son Cory is a personal trainer. He needs his client's complete cooperation for the training to be effective. Clients must show up consistently, work through pain and discomfort, and change their eating habits so they can experience transformation. This workout prepares them to live healthy lives.

In the same way, we get with our own personal trainer, the Holy Spirit. We must make time to "work out" with Him and receive fresh grace every day. We engage in the practices that will retrain our minds and bodies in regards to our new hearts. We will look at some of these practices in Chapter 4.

We can be empowered to face life situations and experience the fruit of the Spirit, such as joy, peace, and self-control. Some of us have some bad habits that are still present in our bodies or in our minds. This does not mean we do not have new hearts or that part of our old hearts remains. It does not mean that God is mad at us or that we are a failure and should just give up.

We do need to be intentional about learning new habits, learning how to live with our new hearts with the help of our personal trainer, the Holy Spirit. Christian growth does not happen because we work hard to get something we don't have. But it does depend on our choosing the "hard work" to live in the reality of what we already do have—new hearts—thanks to our Donor, Jesus. Paul encouraged new believers:

Therefore, my beloved, as you have always obeyed, not as in my presence only, but now much more in my absence, work out your own salvation with fear and trembling; for it is God who works in you both to will and to do for His good pleasure (Philippians 2:12-13).

It is not about earning God's grace, but about our efforts to learn to live with our new hearts. God, the Holy Spirit, is working in us, "both to will and do for His good pleasure." He is a true Helper in this new life. He will never leave or abandon us. No matter what. He stays and helps us through all our hard stuff and challenges. The Holy Spirit enables us to live as righteous children of God, overflowing with the fruits of love, joy, peace, and so much more. The Holy Spirit empowers us to help others, too. This is the most exciting life ever. This is a life of freedom and joyous fellowship. This is a life that reflects the nature and character of God to all those around us. This is the Spirit-filled life we will continue to explore in the remaining chapters of this book.

Thank You, Holy Spirit

Thank You, Holy Spirit for showing us who You are—a loving, Triune God—Father, Son, and Holy Spirit. And thank You for showing us who we are—born-again, righteous sons and daughters of God Himself, restored to our original innocence and image as Your children, because Jesus took our mess and our death. Thank You that You are our Helper, a gift from Jesus to live inside us. Thank You that You never leave us and You personally train us to live this new life.

We have so much more to learn. Thank You for wooing us. Thank You for knowing each one of us personally and leading us into the experience of this new life. We are eager to know more of what You do.

REFLECT on the SPIRIT's WORK in YOUR LIFE

- What were your earliest views of God? Of Jesus? Of the Holy Spirit?

- When did God become more than just a word to you?

- When did you first become aware of your need to be born again? Describe this experience.

- What is one difference that being born again has made in your life?

- What does it mean to you that you are a righteous child of God?

RESPOND to the SPIRIT'S WORK in YOUR LIFE

- If you have not experienced the new birth, why not right now? Simply say, "I believe, Jesus," or I want to know You, Jesus."

- What are some struggles that you need the Spirit's help for?

- What are some new habits you want to adopt to strengthen your new heart?

RELATE to the SPIRIT'S WORK in OTHER'S LIVES

- Watch Rich share his story of seeking the Holy Spirit on the accompanying DVD.

- Discuss your responses with the small group.

Chapter Two:
Help! What Do You Do, Holy Spirit?

The Holy Spirit wants to help us powerfully and practically in our everyday lives and challenges. But first, He wants to make sure we know the truth—about Jesus, life, love, and the approval of the Father. He reveals truth that sets us free!

How would you respond if someone surprised you with the gift of a personal assistant—someone to run your mundane errands, clean your house, care for your children, arrange appointments, and bring you take-out? Or perhaps you prefer more of a life coach, psychotherapist, tutor, or seasoned counselor? Most of us would welcome help with our busy lives. We are often overwhelmed with the cares and concerns of each day. Many live for the weekend, only to be inundated with household tasks, children's sports, the weekly trip to Costco, an overgrown yard, and, of course, getting to church. Help!

God Offers Us Himself

While God does not offer us a personal assistant, permanent babysitter, or lifestyle manager, and He does not specialize in home repairs or car maintenance, He does offer us a gift that fills our lives with incredible peace, wisdom, and joy. This changes how we handle those pressing needs and alters the end result in our lives and our families. God offers us the Helper Himself, the Holy Spirit, God's gift of live-in help.

The Holy Spirit has quite the job description. For starters, He has several titles (Teacher of Truth, Comforter, and Advocate are just a few of them); plus, He is the one responsible for gifts of miracles, healing, prophecy, and other amazing supernatural works. Then there are all the byproducts, or "fruit," of His presence in us: love, joy, peace, kindness, and goodness—just to name a few.

100 Percent Free for Eternity

Who wouldn't want all of this help? I think most of us would say "yes," but we are unsure how it works. Is there something we have to do to earn this help or pay for it? Absolutely not! This gift is 100 percent free and comes with an eternal guarantee of abundance and success. God does not fail.

How do we access all that the Holy Spirit does? It seems almost too good to be true that the God of the Universe, the Almighty Creator, would come to live inside human beings, ready to help with all of life. How do we receive God's gift and then live in the fullness of this? Good questions. There are some things we first need to understand, but ultimately, we simply believe.

Guilty Pleasures

I lived much of my life in a battle with guilt and shame. Oh, I had no ugly secret sin like adultery or hatred. But I, a mature Christian, had some secret pleasures that plagued me with guilt. What were these secret pleasures? A long walk on a crisp fall day, admiring the beauty of Midwestern maples turning brilliant red. A second cup of steaming coffee while I soaked in the early morning quiet of a soon-to-be noisy household. An hour lost in the tumultuous world of an intriguing novel. What? Why would such harmless activities blanket me with guilt and rob me of pleasure? Why? Because I believed these were not "spiritual activities" and as such, took me away from more important, more spiritual things like studying my Bible, praying for a sick friend, or writing my next sermon. Hence, I concluded that God was not pleased with my wasting precious time doing selfish things that were not advancing the Kingdom of God.

The Holy Spirit Loves Our Whole Life

Then I discovered that the Holy Spirit loves my *whole* life and was Himself enjoying these secret pleasures of mine, right along with me! It has taken a while for me to absorb this truth, but the guilt is gone.

> It may come as a shock to you, too, that the Holy Spirit is interested in your whole life—from the tedious parenting to the tremendous prayer time to the tough challenges at work to the tempting binge (Netflix or Nutella, or perhaps Netflix plus Nutella?). The Holy Spirit is our Helper. He is ready to help, not hit us over the head!

It may come as a shock to you, too, that the Holy Spirit is interested in your whole life—from the tedious parenting to the tremendous prayer time to the tough challenges at work to the tempting binge (Netflix or Nutella, or perhaps Netflix *plus* Nutella?). The Holy Spirit is our Helper. He is ready to help, not hit us over the head!

A Common Divide

It is quite common in American Christianity to divide our lives into spiritual and unspiritual, into sacred and secular, with the belief that God is not involved or interested in the secular or unspiritual aspects. We think He really cares about our church attendance, Bible reading, and prayer, but He is not so interested when it comes to attendance at the soccer game, reading the newspaper, or conversations with friends. Nothing could be further from the truth! The unspiritual or secular aspects of our lives take up about 90 percent of our days, and trust me, the Holy Spirit wants to be involved, and He is very interested. And I don't mean He is only interested in correcting us or rebuking us for having too much fun at the game or for struggling to not gossip with friends. No! The Holy Spirit wants to help us enjoy all of life and have energy for the fight and for the fun. He is God's gift of live-in help for all of life, every day in every way. My friend Anita had a delightful discovery of this truth, thanks to the Holy Spirit.

The Holy Spirit Loves to Help

"I failed again," Anita sobbed as I put my arm around her. "I'm so stupid! Why did I think I could ever be a doctor?" She covered her face with her hands and shook with despair. I quietly began to pray:

> *"Father, thank You for giving Anita Your Holy Spirit inside of her. Thank You that You are the all-knowing, all-wise God who created the universe, our brains, and our bodies. Thank You, Holy Spirit, that You bring all things to our minds when needed. Now, I ask You to do this for Anita as she prepares for and takes her next medical exam. I ask that You empower her to pass this exam with Your help. In Jesus's Name, Amen."*

Six weeks later Anita ran up to me beaming, exclaiming, "I passed! I'm going to be a doctor!" Yes, I was super happy for her, but I was not surprised. This is what the Holy Spirit loves to do. He loves to help with all of life, and helping with tests is one of His specialties. After all, He is God. He is the most brilliant Being in the Universe. He has been given to us to teach us all truth and bring it to our minds as needed. This is especially helpful for students—young and old—but is great for all types of learning.

"But," you might say, as many have said to me before, "doesn't that just mean the Holy Spirit will teach us the Bible?" Well, of course we need Him to teach us the Bible. It is one of the most important things the Holy Spirit does, and I am so thankful for that. The Bible is pretty darn hard to understand at times. Even with a master's degree in education and 15 hours towards a doctorate, I could never really understand the Bible until I invited the Holy Spirit to be my teacher.

Mental Challenges

Yes, He helps us understand our daily Bible reading, but He is also great at helping us with daily mental challenges: how to breastfeed our fussy newborn, how to balance a complicated budget, how to find our lost keys or how to fix the leaky faucet—we need lots of help. Why are we so used to handling these mental challenges on our own? Why do we look every other place or to every other person except the Spirit of Truth who lives inside us?

Just Ask Him

I have found the Holy Spirit is willing, ready, and able to partner with us in all of life. We only need to ask. Just this week an older single mom shared how frustrated she was with her five-year-old who has ADD (Attention Deficit Disorder). After another tense morning of chaos, she yelled at her daughter, ending with "Help, God!" Suddenly a solution popped in her mind and she was amazed at the simplicity of it. The Holy Spirit is ready to help.

Welcome Him as Helper for math, motherhood, or messes of any kind! After all, He is live-in help. We simply believe this, and then we get quiet long enough to hear Him speak.

The Holy Spirit Dismantles Dualism

Because many of us live compartmentalized, non-integrated lives, it is good to ask the Holy Spirit to help us dismantle all that dualistic thinking and compartmentalization of our lives and prepare for a delightful adventure. This is much easier said than done, I will warn you. Many of us have very strong "religious spirits"—so to speak—that love to shame, condemn, and smother us with guilt for enjoying life too much. Hence, we live miserable lives, always waiting for the other shoe to drop if we are having just a bit too much fun.

Or we think God is mad at us when we fail to "get our act together" or are struggling to balance all the stuff on our plates. We have been taught that the Christian life is sober and serious and that vigilance is critical as we pare down our lives to only the most "holy" to please God. Well, the Holy Spirit Himself, the Spirit of Truth, could not disagree more. Thankfully, He has been given to lead and guide us into real truth, all truth:

> *When the Spirit of truth comes, He will guide you into all the truth, for He will not speak on His own authority, but whatever He hears He will speak, and He will declare to you the things that are to come (John 16:13 ESV).*

The Spirit of truth guides us into all truth. He exposes lies and wrong beliefs. This is one of the most important things the Holy Spirit does. This affects everything. And this is where many of us have gotten off-track and why the Spirit is so important for us. To live in the fullness of all that Jesus intended and made possible, we need the help of the Holy Spirit to lead us into all truth about all of life. Our beliefs make a big difference in how we live.

The Supernatural Has Come

Jesus was clear that He brought the powerful, miraculous rule of God, the Kingdom, to earth. Jesus wasted no time demonstrating the truth of this: gallons of ordinary water turned into the most delicious wine, thousands fed at a huge picnic from a meager five fish and two loaves of bread, hospital-sized crowds of sick and demonized instantly healed, despised sinners embraced and forgiven, and even the stone-cold dead brought back to life! Wherever Jesus showed up, marvelous, life-changing things happened. The Kingdom of God had come. Powerful change was now possible. People were not left to their own devices. God was visiting His people... and the best news: He is still here!

Jesus is all about bringing freedom, abundance, healing, and hope to lives now and forever. Jesus cares about every detail of our lives here on earth and yes, of course, in all eternity, too. He wants us to see, believe, and embrace His help all day long.

For now, ask the Holy Spirit to dismantle any dualistic thinking you have and to reveal to you how much the Spirit wants to help with your life in ordinary and sometimes in unexplainable ways, too. He leads and guides us into all truth.

He is a Great Attorney!

Jesus knew we would need help discerning lies from the enemy and the truth of who we are as a new creation, loved deeply by our Father. So, Jesus made a special request:

> *And I will ask the Father, and He will give you another Advocate (Helper) who will never leave you. He is the Holy Spirit, who leads into all truth (John 14:16-17a).*

Here Jesus calls the Holy Spirit our Advocate. Wow! We have our own personal attorney, one who advocates for and defends us. Why is this so important?

Flat-lined Faith

Christians have a very real enemy named Satan who is also known as the fa-ther of lies and the accuser. He continually spouts lies, distorting the truth to malign our character and God's. This means we are regularly hearing accusa-tions against us like "You are not good enough" or "You are so worthless" or "You are such a failure" or "God is so disappointed in you, again!" or "This mess is impossible to change."

> These accusations and lies hinder—no, they flatline our faith, resulting in dead faith. This sends us into a spiral of doubt and depression. We are stripped of joy, peace, and hope. The Spirit of Truth, our Advocate, expos-es these statements as lies and false accusations from Satan. He then reminds us of the truth.

These accusations and lies hinder—no, they flatline our faith, resulting in dead faith. This sends us into a spiral of doubt and depression. We are stripped of joy, peace, and hope. The Spirit of Truth, our Advocate, exposes these state-ments as lies and false accusations from Satan. He then reminds us of the truth. It is up to us to receive this truth into our hearts and as Paul says, be:

Renewed in the spirit of our mind (Ephesians 4:23 NKJV).

This is a marvelous work of our Helper, the Holy Spirit! It is more than mem-orizing some Bible verses although that is important. The Holy Spirit brings a transformation at a much deeper level than mere intellectual consent. He moves truth from our heart to our head (not from our head to heart)!

It is Better for Me to Go

It is very, very strange, in light of all the marvelous things He did, that Jesus would make the following statement regarding the Holy Spirit:

Nevertheless, I tell you the truth: it is to your advantage that I go away, for if I do not go away, the Helper will not come to you. But if I go, I will send Him to you (John 16:7 ESV).

Say what? To our advantage that Jesus go away? How can that be? Yet, Jesus is clear that it is somehow better for us that the Helper, the Holy Spirit, comes to us than it is for Jesus to remain here on earth. Jesus went on to explain why:

> *And when He (the Holy Spirit) comes, He will convict the world concerning sin and righteousness and judgment: concerning sin, because they do not believe in Me; concerning righteousness, because I go to the Father, and you will see Me no longer; concerning judgment, because the ruler of this world is judged (John 16:8-11 ESV).*

At first glance, this doesn't sound so great (sin, judgment, conviction!) ... or does it? First, Jesus did say that it is better for Him to go so the Holy Spirit can come and be our Helper. Jesus says this is clearly to our advantage. But what is the help He brings? His very important task is to make sure we know the Good News about Jesus—the truth. Jesus knew this would be twisted by religion (and Satan, of course), and history has proven this to be so.

Divine Detective?

Sadly, based on this verse, the church has for years taught that the Holy Spirit is like a Divine Detective of Sin whose main job is to daily troll our hearts and minds to convict us of sin. To be sure we get the message, the religious authorities adamantly say that the Holy Spirit will also rebuke us for our failure to live righteously and will stir up real fear of the impending judgment so we can get our act together and do better tomorrow. Yikes! This sounds miserable to me. I think I want to run and hide from this so-called Helper who is always ready to hit me over the head or punch me in my heart! How can this be to our advantage? This is not to our advantage—because that is *not* what Jesus meant. However, it is the experience of many.

This was basically my experience as I battled guilt for enjoying "selfish" activities that stole precious time I could be using to do ministry. I even asked the Holy Spirit every night to convict me of my sins and my failures, and judge me so I could do better. Each morning I revisited my shame and asked the Spirit to "search me for sin." Even when I could not think of anything, I prayed:

How can I know all the sins lurking in my heart? Cleanse me from these hidden faults. Keep your servant from deliberate sins! Don't let them control me. Then I will be free of guilt and innocent of great sin (Psalm 19:12-13 NLT).

I scolded myself, "Shame on you! Stop sinning, confess your sins, do right or be judged." I was pathetically "sin-focused," while my Savior and His Spirit longed to give me a new set of glasses to see the truth and help me be "Son-focused"!

Faith in Jesus's Work, Not Our Work

Those new "Son Glasses," given to me by the Spirit, helped me see the truth of what Jesus meant about the advantage we now have with the Spirit as our Helper. First, Jesus said the Spirit would convict the *world* (not devoted disciples) of sin, because they do not believe in Jesus. The Holy Spirit wants to constantly show all people (especially the world) that it is *by faith in Jesus* we are made new. It is not by our strict adherence to a religious code of conduct or by being "right" in all we say and do or by cleaning up our act. No! The glorious Gospel is that Jesus took our sin and offers us His righteousness—it is faith in His work, not ours. He rose from the dead, ascended to the Father, and gives us the gift of His righteousness so we now can reflect Jesus to all!

Satan Judged, Not Us

The Holy Spirit wants to make sure we know that the ruler of this world, Satan, has been judged and is rendered defeated. Jesus made that happen at the cross and resurrection. Yay! Jesus took the judgment for us. He is no longer judging us. Thank you, Holy Spirit! You unveil the glory of Jesus to the world. You convict people of unbelief in Jesus. You show us His righteousness and His defeat of Satan. This is really Good News. Thank you for showing us the true Gospel. We can now believe this wonderful truth about Jesus and all He has done. We are no longer sin-focused. We are Son-focused.

> The Holy Spirit is not, contrary to popular teaching, a Divine Detective of Sin, but a Bold Deliverer of the Truth: Jesus's Victory over sin, self, and Satan for us! This is such a wonderful work of the Spirit. We can make a choice to live with a fresh assurance from the Spirit that He is leading us into all truth—about Jesus.

Bold Deliverer of the Truth

The Holy Spirit is not, contrary to popular teaching, a Divine Detective of Sin, but a Bold Deliverer of the Truth: Jesus's Victory over sin, self, and Satan for us! This is such a wonderful work of the Spirit. We can make a choice to live with a fresh assurance from the Spirit that He is leading us into all truth—about Jesus. He shows us how much the Father loves us, not beats us up every day, rebuking us for our sin. No, Jesus, our righteousness, has taken sin away, and the Father wants us to live in the sweetness of knowing we are His beloved children.

True Identity

Five-year-olds Bobby and Billy literally crawled on all fours into the special education classroom where I worked one summer. They did not speak any words, but only emitted soft barking sounds. They recoiled at my touch and had no idea how to take and eat the graham crackers I offered. What had happened to them? Child protective services had rescued them out of a home where they had been caged and treated like dogs. No wonder they had no idea how to respond as human beings! It was such a privilege and joy to watch them discover their true identity that summer. Knowing they were precious, loved, and wanted little boys, Bobby and Billy blossomed!

We are Much Loved, Righteous Sons and Daughters

I know most of us do not think we are dogs, but we often do not know our true identities as the much-loved, righteous sons and daughters of God, our Father. This is devastating. The Holy Spirit wants to make sure we know and believe our true identities. No one is left as an orphan. We are all adopted. This is one of the Holy Spirit's very important assignments. We can struggle with truly believing that we have been made sons and daughters of the Father right now with full benefits and privileges and blessings and are no longer slaves, servants, or orphans, working hard for acceptance and approval. I have listed on the Resources page several great books that address Orphan Thinking.

"Papa!"

The Spirit wants to release the "Papa, Daddy" cry in all of our hearts, assuring us that we are no longer slaves, but full heirs of our loving Father, who paid a huge price for us to be reconciled to Him. He is the One who works in our hearts so we can say confidently and intimately to God, "Papa, Daddy," or, as the Bible records in Aramaic, "Abba."

> So you have not received a spirit that makes you fearful slaves. Instead, you received God's Spirit when He adopted you as His own children. Now we call Him, "Abba, Father." For His Spirit joins with our spirit to affirm that we are God's children (Romans 8:51-16 NLT).

How does He do this? How does the Spirit assure each person that he or she is greatly loved and accepted and uniquely created by the heavenly Father? How is each person convinced that the Father adopted him or her as His own child?

For every person it will differ, because everyone comes from a different life situation. But the end result is that everyone lives gloriously without fear and with the full assurance of the Father's love and acceptance as His precious child, chosen, adopted, and deeply loved. When this is settled, almost all aspects of one's life are healthy and whole. Actually, I dare to say, all aspects of one's life are healthy and whole when you know that NOTHING (no sin, no failure, no tragedy, no devil) can separate you from the Father's love. This is what Paul wrote to the Romans:

> And I am convinced that nothing can ever separate us from God's love. Neither death nor life, neither angels nor demons neither our fears for today nor our worries about tomorrow—not even the powers of hell can separate us from God's love. No power in the sky above or in the earth below—indeed, nothing in all creation will ever be able to separate us from the love of God that is revealed in Christ Jesus our Lord (Romans 8:38-39 NLT).

The Holy Spirit is eager to make this a reality in your life. He knows your past. He has a great future for you. He delights to convince you of the Father's love, whereby you can confidently call out "Daddy." He knows that Jesus has made all of this possible at a very great price.

Heritage of Faith

I am thankful for having a wonderful, Christian home with godly parents who still love each other and love Jesus even at their present age of 90. That is a tremendous heritage. My father was a business owner who worked hard, long hours every day except Sunday. Because he was a lay minister in our church, he was also busy on Sundays—preaching sermons, visiting the sick in hospitals, and being available for people in the church family. Ours was a tight-knit, loving, but very strict religious community. No nonsense was tolerated. Likewise, my dad, being of German blood, was stern and reserved in his lifestyle and in expressing his emotions. Yet there was never any doubt he deeply loved my five siblings and me. He showed us his affection by his ample provision, his absolute commitment to my mom, and by taking us all on fun, family summer trips to practically every state in the USA. However, his ascetic faith would not allow him to attend many of our school functions, nor could he show any interest in the arts, theater, dance, or sporting events. This was difficult for me. I did not fit the religious mold for women at all. I was dramatic, emotional, bold, and a leader. I loved music, dancing, and the stage. The message I received (although never spoken directly to me) was that I, daring, dramatic Dianne, was a disappointment to my dad.

Father God is Not Disappointed

As is often the case, I transferred this daddy disappointment to Father God. Although I knew in my head that was not true and indeed, the Father loved me unconditionally, my heart was heavy with a dark sense of disappointment. I have since learned that when people are asked, "How do you think God feels about you?" one of the most common responses is "I think He is pretty disappointed!" Maybe you can relate to that sentiment.

> He showed me plainly that neither I, nor anyone else for that matter, needed a perfect earthly father to have a healthy relationship with the Father in heaven. If that were so, we would all be in trouble.

No Perfect Fathers

One of the first things the Spirit of Truth did to repair my Father relationship was to show me some important truths. He showed me plainly that neither I, nor anyone else for that matter, needed a perfect earthly father to have a healthy relationship with the Father in heaven. If that were so, we would all be in trouble. I am pretty sure most families have major dysfunction when it comes to both father and mother. In addition, while much psychotherapy, counseling, and prayer focuses on addressing past parental issues, much of that can fall short of strengthening us in our relationship with the Father.

I think we can try to strengthen relationships with our parents. Life is so much happier when these are healthy. If you hold grudges or have bitterness towards your father or mother (I understand there can be real reason for this), you should ask the Spirit to impart the gift of forgiveness to give to them. As you freely forgive them (whether they are still alive or not), you can be set free from any unforgiveness, which is so destructive. When this happens, you are often given new perspective into why your parents did what they did (I am not referring to very sinful actions, such as abuse).

New Perspective

For example, I was able to see that the reason my father did not attend any of my drama or marching squad functions was not because he was ashamed or because he disapproved of me, but because he was a man who honored his church commitments as a minister. These commitments did not allow him to attend such events. While I did not agree with or like this, I was blessed that he was a man of integrity and honor despite my own disappointment. It was not me he was disappointed in, although it felt that way at the time.

Jesus is the Way to the Father

These perspectives are healing and helpful. The Holy Spirit as the Spirit of Truth is so faithful to reveal where we have not believed the truth. We want to have the healthiest relationship possible with both our earthly father and our heavenly Father. But, I want to reiterate that it is not our earthly fathers who are the way to the Father. The Holy Spirit made it so clear to me that cleaning up all my "father messes" is not the way to knowing and experiencing the Father's love for me. This is so important.

Jesus alone is the way to the Father—in more dimensions than just a general saving one. Jesus said if we have seen Him, we have seen the Father. If we want to know what the Father is like, how to relate to the Father, how to experience the Father's love, we need to look at Jesus. And trust Jesus in us by His Spirit to unveil the Father.

> *Jesus told him, "I am the way, the truth, and the life. No one can come to the Father except through Me. If you had really known Me, you would know who My Father is. From now on, you do know Him and have seen Him!"*
>
> *Philip said, "Lord, show us the Father, and we will be satisfied." Jesus replied, "Have I been with you all this time, Philip, and yet you still don't know who I am? Anyone who has seen Me has seen the Father! So why are you asking Me to show Him to you?*
>
> *Don't you believe that I am in the Father and the Father is in Me? The words I speak are not My own, but My Father who lives in Me does His work through Me. Just believe that I am in the Father and the Father is in Me" (John 14:6-11 NLT).*

This is the same relational union into which we are invited. Jesus shows us a merciful, miracle-working, loving Father who longs to lavish love and blessing on His children. If you want to know the Father, say to Jesus, "Show me the Father. I want to be fully saturated with the Father's love for me. I want to know I am not a disappointing daughter or son. I believe You."

Our New Identity

This brings me back to Jesus, what He did for me and who He has made me. The Spirit helps me to know I am so valuable, so loved, and so priceless, that Jesus would die for me to make me new and give me a new identity. I am made in His image, filled with Him, and in union with Him. I am no longer a sinner. I am a saint. I am blameless and holy in His sight. I am 100 percent righteous with His righteousness. I am a holy, clean, new temple—the perfect home for Him. I choose to believe this and not go by my feelings, which can fluctuate with the weather and with what I ate for dinner. I choose to believe this no matter how good or how bad my relationship is with my earthly father. I believe.

> The Holy Spirit longs to fully form Christ in us. He does not want us searching for a false self or an old self or even a new self. He wants us to be who God our Father created us uniquely to be. He helps us to believe.

Jesus Wants Us Whole

I am not negative toward inner healing prayer (which often focuses on the father issue) if it is about Jesus and the truth and moves us forward and not backward. Such prayer helps if the Spirit is exposing lies that we have believed about Jesus, His finished work, or ourselves as a new creation in Christ. We can, with the Spirit's power and help, see the truth, repent for believing lies, and walk in the wholeness and holiness Jesus paid for us to have and which the Spirit makes real in our lives.

However, inner healing and introspection do NOT help if you are going to dig up past hurts or try to fix a dead person—which is what the old you is. It is like trying to put makeup on a corpse or talking to the dead. This is self-obsessed and sin-focused and not Savior- and Spirit-focused at all. Remember, we have been crucified and raised with Christ. Learning to live in the truth of this is absolutely critical. The Holy Spirit longs to fully form Christ in us. He does not want us searching for a false self or an old self or even a new self. He wants us to be who God our Father created us uniquely to be. He helps us to believe.

Thank You for All You Do, Holy Spirit

There is so much more I could say about all that the Holy Spirit does in and through us. For now, I thank Him for dismantling the dualism in our lives and showing us how much He wants to help with everything. He leads us into all truth about God, revealing how much He loves us and redeemed our innocence through Jesus's victorious work over sin, death, and Satan. He assures us we are much-loved sons and daughters who have intimacy with the Father, whom we call "Daddy," knowing nothing can separate us from His love.

REFLECT *on the* SPIRIT'S WORK *in* YOUR LIFE

- What has been your experience of dividing your life into spiritual/unspiritual? Share experiences of ignorance, guilt, shame, etc., and any sense of the Spirit's help.

- What has been your experience of the Spirit as a Divine Detective? Deliverer of Truth? Do you identify more with being a sinner or a saint? Explain.

- How have you been more of an orphan than a son or daughter? How do you feel about calling God "Daddy" or "Papa"?

- Have you felt you were a disappointing child to your earthly father? Heavenly Father? Share how this impacted you.

RESPOND *to the* SPIRIT'S WORK *in* YOUR LIFE

- The Holy Spirit dismantles dualism. Ask the Holy Spirit to help you dismantle the dualism in your life. Note where this is most needed.

- The Holy Spirit helps with ordinary problems. Right now, ask the Holy Spirit to help you with an ordinary problem. Listen for what pops in your head.

- The Holy Spirit reveals Jesus and His work. Share the truth about Jesus in your own words.

- The Holy Spirit reveals "Papa." Share about your relationship with God as Father. How has your earthy father influenced this?

RELATE *to the* SPIRIT'S WORK *in* OTHER'S LIVES

- Watch Tosha share her story of seeking the Holy Spirit on the accompanying DVD.

- Discuss your responses with the small group.

Chapter Three:
Help! How Do I
Encounter You,
Holy Spirit?

There is an encounter with the Holy Spirit, accompanied
by actual experiences, that is available for all.
These experiences may include the gift of tongues, physical
sensations, the gift of prophecy, fresh desire to worship, the
gift of powerful witnessing, and greater understanding of the
Bible. When we encounter God, something happens!

On May 5, 1977, the Bible seemed frustrating and irrelevant to me. I needed a miracle, but I was told that the miracles of the Bible had ceased. On
May 6, 1977, scales fell off my eyes and I saw the Bible clearly revealed that
Jesus is still doing miracles. On May 5, 1977, I said I would never speak
in tongues. I was taught that this practice was evil at worst, and just plain
weird at best. On May 6, 1977, I spoke in tongues for the first time and
have cherished this life-changing (and yes, somewhat weird) gift ever since.
On May 5, 1977, even though I had been a committed disciple of Jesus's for
over five years, I rarely shared my faith. I was taught one should just "let

your light shine through good deeds and a holy lifestyle." On May 6, 1977, I could not wait to shout, "Jesus is alive and still doing miracles!" I have not stopped shouting about—and seeing—Jesus doing miracles for four decades. On May 5, 1977, I solemnly sang hymns from a hymnbook without any instrumental accompaniment. I was taught instrumentation was "not Biblical" in a church setting. On May 6, 1977, I released a cry of praise and worship that has now been accompanied by a full band every week, in and out of church, usually without a hymnbook (although those old hymns have truly come alive to me now).

Radical Encounter

What happened on May 6, 1977, that so radically changed my life? Simply put, I encountered the Holy Spirit, up close and personal, or as the Bible says, I was "baptized in the Holy Spirit." Jesus told his disciples:

John baptized with water, but in just a few days you will be baptized with the Holy Spirit (Acts 1:5 ESV).

I had been baptized in water five years earlier and understood this term *baptize* meant "to be immersed, overwhelmed." However, I was unsure what this meant in reference to the Holy Spirit. On May 5, I heard a speaker teach on being baptized in the Holy Spirit. I was stirred to have my own personal encounter with this Holy Spirit, although I knew nothing about Him, except for a rare (and hesitant) reference to Him by my pastor. I was skeptical and scared for sure. It was all so different from what I had been taught, and I was nervous about being deceived or just being plain stupid—both big concerns for someone like me who liked to rationally understand all things and keep them under control.

At just past midnight on May 6, I was unable to sleep and sensed a deep desire to encounter the Holy Spirit as I heard described. I descended from my upstairs bedroom to the first-floor office of our traditional Cape Cod home. Hoisting my ankle-length, lace-trimmed nightgown, I knelt by the hide-a-bed sofa. The loud thumping of my heart contrasted eerily with the dark stillness of this moonlit night. As I knelt there, I recalled what I had read in a small booklet I picked up at that meeting. The author had referenced a Scripture about the Spirit in the Gospel of John:

On the last day, that great day of the feast, Jesus stood and cried out, saying, "If anyone thirsts, let him come to Me and drink. He who believes in Me, as the Scripture has said, out of his heart (belly) will flow rivers of living water." But this He spoke concerning the Spirit, whom those believing in Him would receive; for the Holy Spirit was not yet given, because Jesus was not yet glorified (John 7:37-39 NKJV).

Yes, I was thirsty to encounter the Spirit. Did I understand this verse? No, not really. I was not sure how to "come to Him," as Jesus said, and it did not make much sense. But the booklet said to place your hand on your belly and ask Jesus to baptize (immerse) you in the Holy Spirit like a river of living water. Then, you were to wait with expectation (more like fear, in my case!) for this to happen. I followed the steps exactly as outlined. To my surprise, I had no sooner finished asking Jesus to baptize me when I felt a bubbling sensation rise from my stomach up to my throat. So, I opened my mouth to say thank you to Jesus, but instead, out came a language I had never spoken before in my life. Before I had a chance to figure it all out and control it, or before I had the chance to doubt and argue, I was baptized in the Holy Spirit and speaking in tongues!

God Wants You to Encounter His Spirit

I have since had the privilege of praying for thousands of people to be baptized in the Holy Spirit in exactly the same way as I prayed for myself. I have laid my hands on their bellies. I have watched as the Holy Spirit, this River of Living Water, began to bubble up and gush forth. I have listened in amazement as a stream of speech, an unknown language that is speaking mysteries to God Himself, came forth from people's lips. I have watched the Holy Spirit bring other remarkable changes to peoples' lives—over and over.

When we encounter God, something happens! What is fascinating to me is that scientists have now proven that speaking in tongues is real (although we already knew that!). In a study at the University of Pennsylvania conducted by Dr. Andrew Newberg, researchers took brain images of five women while they spoke in tongues, and found that the language areas—the frontal lobes—were quiet. But the thalamus, where it is believed we have spiritual experiences, showed increased activity. The new languages spoken were highly structured, with clear, articulate phrases, suggesting that the language was being generated in a different way, or coming from another source.

And it was! That source is none other than the Holy Spirit, who has given us spiritual languages to communicate with God.

I never tire of witnessing this miracle of Holy Spirit baptism. Because I know this is God's will for every person, I can pray with faith for each and every one to be immersed in the Holy Spirit and encounter Him. Almost every time (there are a few exceptions), I have seen God answer this prayer quickly, powerfully, and miraculously. Sometimes people are afraid or filled with doubt. I like to reassure them with what the apostle Peter said after thousands were baptized in the Holy Spirit on the Day of Pentecost, as recorded in the Book of Acts:

> *This promise (the Holy Spirit) is to you, to your children, and to those far away—all who have been called by the Lord our God (Acts 2:39 NLT).*

I agree with Peter, and would encourage everyone to be baptized in the Spirit—to encounter Him in an experiential way. I would go so far as to say it is a nonnegotiable encounter if you want to have a deep and lasting relationship with the Holy Spirit and be equipped to do what He calls you to do as Jesus's disciple.

I agree with Peter, and would encourage everyone to be baptized in the Spirit—to encounter Him in an experiential way. I would go so far as to say it is a nonnegotiable encounter if you want to have a deep and lasting relationship with the Holy Spirit and be equipped to do what He calls you to do as Jesus's disciple. But don't compare your encounter with someone else's and wonder if you "measure up"—for sure, everyone's encounter is different, because we are all different.

Brief Church History Lesson

When I received my initial baptism in the Holy Spirit, it was in 1977 during the middle of what is now labeled the Charismatic Movement by church historians. This was an era when many people in mainline denominational churches were experiencing the Holy Spirit for the first time, just as I did. Most of us had never really heard of the Holy Spirit, except in our church creeds or doctrinal statements. Our experience of the Holy Spirit was distinct, sometimes divisive, and always unmistakable. We spoke in tongues, prayed for the sick, danced with tambourines, and prophesied—all things we had never even heard of, let alone done, in our previous practice as Christians. Such new practices resulted in many people leaving (or being excommunicated from) their faith of origin. However, this also brought new life to many church groups, including Catholics, Lutherans, Episcopalians, and Mennonites, to name just a few. Whole congregations of both Catholic and Protestant churches were dynamically renewed during this sovereign move of God's Holy Spirit. I am humbled to have been a part of it. Of course, there were plenty of controversies.

Controversies

One of the bigger controversies arose when the established Pentecostal denominations taught that the baptism of the Spirit was a "second work." People then inferred (whether this was intended or not) that if you did not have the second encounter of a baptism in the Holy Spirit (after being born again), you were a second-class Christian. This resulted in bitter division with other Christian groups. Vineyard Church leader John Wimber helped to heal this division, though much confusion and controversy remain. He taught that all who are born again are already baptized in the Spirit, or immersed into Jesus, at the new birth. But, he continued, we should ask for and receive an activation of the Spirit's Presence—a real, experiential infilling, a fresh baptism, so to speak, because many people were ignorant of the Spirit's Presence in their lives.

Such activation of the Spirit means people experience something—tongues, physical sensations, or other gifts like prophecy, worship, healing, or teaching. This could be experienced as an outpouring or an inpouring of the Spirit. The prepositions—out, in, upon, etc.—do not really matter! What matters? That you know you have encountered the Holy Spirit!

Repeated Infillings

Wimber also taught that people should continue to want, expect, and experience repeated infillings, or immersions, in the Spirit's Presence. Everyone could and should welcome the Spirit's Presence and His gifts, again and again.

So we see that experiencing the Holy Spirit is not just a one-time event. We, like the early disciples, can have multiple infillings. And, yes, we may experience physical manifestations of heat, wind, "drunkenness," and shaking, just like believers in the Book of Acts.

More Than Mental Agreement

The Holy Spirit infilling is not just an act of mental agreement by faith with no visible signs. The Holy Spirit infilling—baptism, zapping, activation, release, encounter (it has been called many things)—is an actual experience and is essential to a vibrant Christian life. This is a teaching that changed me, changed the church, and yes, even changed the world. It is still doing just that!

Don't Put God in a Theological Box

I do not intend to argue for or demand a specific theology in regards to the baptism of the Holy Spirit. There has been much ink spilled over this topic. Of course, I care about sound doctrine and do not want to embrace faulty theology. I am a student of church history and a lover of God's Word. But I defer to God! And God the Holy Spirit delights in surprising us. Such surprises are difficult to receive, much less notice, if one is too engrossed in theological correctness. History testifies to this truth.

> Humble yourself. Be open to however the Holy Spirit wants to encounter you. Trust Him and His many different ways. Don't put God in a theological box. After all, He is God!

Humble yourself. Be open to however the Holy Spirit wants to encounter you. Trust Him and His many different ways. Don't put God in a theological box. After all, He is God!

Diversity of Encounters and Effects

The Bible does illustrate several effects that are typical of being baptized in the Spirit. There is likewise a broad spectrum of ways this happens from person to person or even from group to group. Nevertheless, there are always one or more effects that are experienced—with varying degrees of intensity and frequency—after one encounters the Holy Spirit. Most people experience one or more of the following after an initial baptism in the Spirit:

- Empowering for mission
- Speaking in tongues
- Gift of prophecy
- Understanding the Word
- Freedom in worship

A Necessary Empowering for Mission

"I loved Jesus and had a passion to tell others about Him, but I often felt powerless to do so," lamented Rand, a former college football player who oozed with personal charisma. "I tried hosting Bible studies, prayer times, even hangouts at the local bar, but usually my efforts flopped. That was... until I was baptized in the Holy Spirit—in a bar parking lot, no less! My entire life and ability to witness for Jesus was impacted. While it has been an up-and-down journey, I now travel the world sharing Jesus in power and seeing peoples' lives changed. This cannot be done effectively without the empowering of the Spirit! Jesus was right, wait to be empowered before embarking on your mission."

Yes, Jesus told his disciples to wait to be empowered with the Spirit, and He says the same thing to us, His 21st century disciples. We need the promise of the Father to proclaim and demonstrate the Gospel. Jesus said:

> *And now I will send the Holy Spirit, just as My Father promised. But stay here in the city until the Holy Spirit comes and fills you with power from heaven (Luke 24:49 NLT).*

> *Once when He was eating with them, He commanded them, "Do not leave Jerusalem until the Father sends you the gift He promised, as I told you before. John baptized with water, but in just a few days you will be baptized with the Holy Spirit" (Acts 1:4-5 NLT).*

Jesus Himself said the baptism of the Spirit was an absolute must if His disciples were going to fulfill the mission of being powerful witnesses for Him. They waited the 10 days before the outpouring of the Spirit on the Day of Pentecost, as recorded in Acts 2, and then experienced so much power that those watching thought they were drunk! These disciples and many others continued the same ministry of Jesus with powerful signs:

A deep sense of awe came over them all, and the apostles performed many miraculous signs and wonders (Acts 2:43 NLT).

Such power turned the known world upside down. The disciples, who were baptized in the Holy Spirit, did powerful works in Jesus's name. Today, we do not have to wait. The Spirit has been poured out. We simply receive the baptism or immersion of the Spirit and watch Him motivate us. Is this an option? Well, we always have a choice, so in that sense, yes, it is optional.

The Power Couch

I choose to side with Jesus here. I, like Rand, was an utter failure at sharing the Gospel before I was baptized in the Spirit. I just tried to "let my light shine," and not many noticed!   After my husband and I experienced the Spirit, the small Bible study in our home exploded. Each week, people who were hungry for God sat on our couch, received a baptism in the Spirit, and then dragged a friend to come next week to the "Power Couch." Why had we even attempted being Jesus's witnesses apart from the Holy Spirit's empowering presence? Our lamps needed to be plugged in to the Power Source for His light to shine through us.

Of course, many have done missions without this full acknowledgment and welcome of the Holy Spirit. And, yes, good results have come. But our hurting world needs to encounter the Living God who still does miracles. People need the power of God to change impossible life situations. We will explore more of this in Chapter 6, where we learn to naturally and supernaturally give away the Spirit's gifts to others.

Watch Out for Speaking in Tongues!

"Speaking in tongues is from the devil. Watch out! People who speak in tongues foam at the mouth and speak gibberish!" Such was a popular warning back when I was a teenager, and it continues even now. Imagine my surprise when I found myself doing the very thing I had been warned not to do and then discovered it is a very precious and powerful gift. And, to this date, I have never foamed at the mouth or spoken gibberish.

Supernatural Sign

Tongues simply means *language*, and this can be a known or unknown language. When the Spirit was first poured out on Pentecost, those who spoke in tongues spoke languages that they did not personally know, but the listeners did. This was a powerful supernatural sign, as the speakers praised God in languages the foreigners present could understand. This has since been repeated many times all over the world. Yet, speaking in tongues remains a controversial and confusing gift of the Spirit. Check out one of the listed resources for a more detailed treatment. For our purposes, I want to establish that this is a Biblical effect of encountering the Holy Spirit, just as happened to the early disciples of Jesus:

> *While Apollos was in Corinth, Paul traveled through the interior regions until he reached Ephesus, on the coast, where he found several believers. "Did you receive the Holy Spirit when you believed?" he asked them. "No," they replied, "we haven't even heard that there is a Holy Spirit." "Then what baptism did you experience?" he asked. And they replied, "The baptism of John." Paul said, "John's baptism called for repentance from sin. But John himself told the people to believe in the one who would come later, meaning Jesus." As soon as they heard this, they were baptized in the name of the Lord Jesus. Then when Paul laid his hands on them, the Holy Spirit came on them, and they spoke in other tongues and prophesied (Acts 19:1-6 NLT).*

Other accounts in Acts also show believers received the gift of speaking in tongues when they encountered the Holy Spirit. This was especially notable in Peter's retelling of the event in Acts 11, when the non-Jewish people heard the Gospel for the first time, and boom! They were baptized in the Holy Spirit:

> *"As I began to speak," Peter continued, "the Holy Spirit fell on them, just as He fell on us at the beginning. Then I thought of the Lord's words when He said, 'John baptized with water, but you will be baptized with the Holy Spirit.' And since God gave these Gentiles the same gift He gave us when we believed in the Lord Jesus Christ, who was I to stand in God's way?" (Acts 11:15-17 NLT).*

Speaking Intimately with God

This gift is especially helpful for strengthening our intimacy with God. We can share our hearts with God when we do not have our own words. Paul described it this way in a letter to the Corinthians:

> *If you praise Him (God) in the private language of tongues, God understands you but no one else does, for you are sharing intimacies just between you and Him.*
>
> *I'm grateful to God for the gift of praying in tongues that He gives us for praising Him, which leads to wonderful intimacies we enjoy with Him. I enter into this as much or more than any of you (1 Corinthians 14:2, 18 MSG).*

Speaking in tongues is a wonderful, diverse gift that is available for all who desire it. It is not a badge of maturity or elitism. It is a gift I have treasured for 40 years and am convinced the Father delights in giving to any who ask.

Throughout church history, some denominations have insisted that speaking in tongues is the only real sign of the baptism of the Spirit, while others (Vineyard included) contended that it was one of various ways the Holy Spirit may be encountered and experienced, but not the only way nor the absolute necessary way. Speaking in tongues is a wonderful, diverse gift that is available for all who desire it. It is not a badge of maturity or elitism. It is a gift I have treasured for 40 years and am convinced the Father delights in giving to any who ask.

The Ability to Prophesy

"I always thought that only the super spiritual people had the ability to prophesy," said Charlotte, a petite mother of five who has her hands full with mundane, seemingly unspiritual tasks. "I would stand in awe as these spiritual giants said wonderful things to others and brought so much encouragement with powerful words that sounded like God was speaking directly. Then, I was taught that *all* could prophesy. And this included me—

little, ordinary, spiritual grasshopper me! I have since been trained and now train others to give away this life-changing gift to friends, family and yes, even to strangers. Everyone needs encouragement from God."

Speak Words from God

Another effect of being baptized in the Holy Spirit is the gift of prophecy. This is exactly what the prophet Joel predicted and what Peter reminded the crowd who witnessed the first baptism in the Spirit:

> *These people are not drunk, as some of you are assuming. Nine o'clock in the morning is much too early for that. No, what you see was predicted long ago by the prophet Joel:*

> *"In the last days," God says, "I will pour out my Spirit upon all people. Your sons and daughters will prophesy. Your young men will see visions, and your old men will dream dreams. In those days I will pour out My Spirit even on My servants—men and women alike— and they will prophesy" (Acts 2:15-18 NLT).*

Prophecy is simply the ability from the Holy Spirit to speak words from God that encourage, motivate, comfort, and challenge others. This is a precious gift of the Spirit, and Paul the apostle says we should desire it:

> *Let love be your highest goal! But you should also desire the special abilities the Spirit gives—especially the ability to prophesy.*

> *But one who prophesies strengthens others, encourages them, and comforts them (1 Corinthians 14:1, 3 NLT).*

Everyone Can Prophesy

Everyone can learn to flow in this powerful gift that truly blesses those around us, even strangers. Just recently a young man in our city was eating at a local restaurant when he noticed a young mother nearby, sitting with her daughter and enjoying lunch. He sensed God wanted to speak to her through the gift of prophecy. So, he walked over and simply said, "Hi! Sometimes God gives me insights into people's lives, and today He told me that He wanted you to know He thinks you are a wonderful mother!" Tears spilled down her cheeks. Unknown to the young man, this mother had tragically lost a small child to a traumatic death, and she blamed herself for this. Hearing that God thought she was a wonderful mother, spoken to her by a complete stranger, brought supernatural comfort and encouragement.

Think what an amazing world it would be if we all were eager to share prophecy—words of encouragement, comfort, and strength—to those in our path. Lives would be changed!

Understanding the Word, Loving Jesus

Peter, a doctoral student at the university with a keen mind that demands things make sense, had about given up on reading the Bible. "Then, I encountered the Holy Spirit, and discovered I was reading the Bible in the wrong way," he said. "It isn't a textbook. It isn't even a life instruction manual. The Bible is the story of Jesus—from start to finish. This has made a huge difference in how I read it now, as the Spirit teaches me so many amazing things about Jesus and how to know Him better." Another powerful effect of encountering the Holy Spirit is that one can now understand (and enjoy!) the Bible better. This is because the Spirit reveals the deep things of God, as Paul the apostle tells us:

> But it was to us that God revealed these things by His Spirit. For His Spirit searches out everything and shows us God's deep secrets. No one can know a person's thoughts except that person's own spirit, and no one can know God's thoughts except God's own Spirit. And we have received God's Spirit (not the world's spirit), so we can know the wonderful things God has freely given us (1 Corinthians 2:10-12 NLT).

We can know the wonderful things God has freely given us. Thank You, Holy Spirit! Of course, the favorite activity of the Holy Spirit is to reveal more and more of Jesus to us, both in the Bible and in our lives. Jesus becomes more real and we grow in our love for Him, assured of His love for us. Jesus did tell the Bible scholars of His day that one can read the right book and get the wrong message:

> You search the Scriptures because you think they give you eternal life. But the Scriptures point to Me! (John 5:39 NLT).

Yes, we can search and study the Bible and miss Jesus. Some people are so afraid of deception and getting off track, they are paralyzed and stuck in old thinking that stifles their relationship with Jesus. They may study the Greek and Hebrew and be meticulous about proof texts and "being right" and miss out on the truth that eternal life is knowing Jesus.

> If Jesus is getting bigger, better, and more beautiful, then you do not need to fear that you are being deceived. The Holy Spirit is revealing Jesus, in whom are hidden all the treasures of wisdom and knowledge. Invite the Holy Spirit to open the Word to you, starting with the Living Word, Jesus Christ.

If Jesus is getting bigger, better, and more beautiful, then you do not need to fear that you are being deceived. The Holy Spirit is revealing Jesus, in whom are hidden all the treasures of wisdom and knowledge. Invite the Holy Spirit to open the Word to you, starting with the Living Word, Jesus Christ.

Freedom in Praise and Worship

Charlie is a successful businessman who was raised as a strict, devout Baptist. He was well taught in the proper sobriety of worship, and for many years he endured the boring solemnity that accompanied the church service. His marriage hit a rocky spell, so he left his church and began attending the Vineyard church. Imagine his surprise when, after encountering the Holy Spirit, he found himself clapping along with the drums during the worship time at church. It wasn't long before he was raising his hands and joyfully singing the songs displayed on the screen (not in the hymnbook). Charlie had a refreshing release of joy—one of the indications of an encounter with the Spirit. New freedom in praise and worship is one of the invigorating changes that come with being baptized in the Spirit. Because the Spirit brings such a fresh impartation of God's love and goodness, it is easy to want to shout, clap, and sing joyously. Praising is a natural outflow of being filled with God's Presence. This happened very spontaneously as Peter shared Jesus with non-Jewish people who had very little grid for God:

Even as Peter was saying these things, the Holy Spirit fell upon all who were listening to the message. The Jewish believers who came with Peter were amazed that the gift of the Holy Spirit had been poured out on the Gentiles, too. For they heard them speaking in other tongues and praising God (Acts 10:44-46 NLT).

Again, each person will respond differently to the Spirit's freedom in worship, according to one's own personality and temperament. But be assured, an encounter with the Holy Spirit causes even the most reserved, stoic persons to weep or laugh or simply delight in singing not just *about* God, but also *to* Him. After all, we love Him with all our *hearts*, not just our heads. And that love is physically and emotionally expressed with joy and thankfulness! Any wise wife—and husband, too—knows that about true love.

Encounter Effects Are Essential

Effects are essential. I say this because there is an interesting phenomenon occurring in 2017 that is a bit different from the move of the Spirit in 1977. Forty years later, the Holy Spirit is now common knowledge among most Christians. It is quite fashionable to say one is filled with the Spirit or baptized in the Spirit. Most believers would say this is true of them if asked. However, many of these same people do not actually practice the gifts of the Holy Spirit or any other supernatural element associated with the Holy Spirit, including speaking in tongues, praying regularly for the sick, or prophesying to others. Commenting on this, Ed Stetzer, a leading researcher for LifeWay Research and trusted spokesperson for the church in America, said in the October 17, 2013, edition of *Christianity Today*: "Most people I encounter believe in some form of sign gifts at work today, but they are simply not sure how to apply them. Thus, it seems like a lot of young pastors are what I call 'aspirational charismatics.' They believe in all the gifts, aspire to see them at work, but have not actualized that reality in their own lives and churches."

Be Ready to Receive

My response to this is I encourage these pastors and all others who desire to see the gifts of the Holy Spirit in operation to receive a personal baptism of the Holy Spirit, an actual encounter with the Spirit, and be expectant and eager to speak in tongues, prophesy, praise, and practice other gifts of the Spirit.

Do I think that one must speak in tongues to be baptized in the Spirit? No, but generally speaking, those who do not want this gift or are hesitant to receive it rarely go on to flow in the other sign gifts. This has been my experience in the past 40 years, and many others affirm it.

Indeed, a true experiential encounter with the Holy Spirit can be scary. For many, despite their familiarity with the topic, the subject of the Spirit baptism is still shrouded in skepticism, rationalism, or just plain ignorance. There remains much controversy, division, arguing, and fear of Him.

Forgotten God?

In many ways, the Person of the Holy Spirit is the forgotten Person of our Triune God—Father, Son, and Holy Spirit. Because we humans are familiar with the father/son relationship, we more easily focus on those two Persons of God. We can relate—literally. But, Holy Ghost, Holy Spirit? That can seem weird, elusive, and esoteric, for sure. In 2009, well-known author Francis Chan wrote a book on the Holy Spirit called *Forgotten God*. The book's blurb reads:

> As Jesus ascended into heaven, He promised to send the Holy Spirit—the Helper—so that we could be true and living witnesses for Christ. Unfortunately, today's church has admired the gift but neglected to open it. Francis Chan rips away paper and bows to get at the true source of the church's power—the Holy Spirit. Chan contends that we've ignored the Spirit for far too long, and we are reaping the disastrous results. Thorough scriptural support and compelling narrative form Chan's invitation to stop and remember the One we've forgotten, the Spirit of the living God.

Yes, it is time to remember and then do something about it! Be baptized in the Holy Spirit.

Do not live another day without inviting the Holy Spirit to baptize you—to thoroughly immerse you—in His Presence, blessing you with His gifts, empowering you to be Jesus's disciple.

Challenge and Invitation

I want to challenge you to not just be an "aspiring charismatic." Do not settle for only giving lip service or mental assent to these precious gifts from God. Do not live another day without inviting the Holy Spirit to baptize you—to thoroughly immerse you—in His Presence, blessing you with His gifts, empowering you to be Jesus's disciple. The Spirit wants to encounter you. He wants to show you He is God, and He is ready to change everything in your life for the better.

Best Effect of Encountering the Spirit

What is the most astonishing effect of having received the baptism of the Holy Spirit? Speaking in tongues? No. Healing the sick? No. Prophesying to others? No. Dancing joyously? No. What the Holy Spirit does best is bear witness to Jesus—whether in the Word, experience, or teaching. This is what He first did in my life the morning after I knelt by that sofa in my office and humbled myself to receive the baptism of the Holy Spirit. But this experience is only the beginning of a lifelong, exhilarating relationship with the Person of the Holy Spirit. It will be up to you to pursue this relationship according to your own personality, temperament, and desires. As for His desire—He is longing to live in and through you, moment by moment, every day. He is God's gift of live-in help.

REFLECT *on the SPIRIT'S WORK in YOUR LIFE*

- What are your fears, concerns, or questions about encountering the Holy Spirit in an experiential way?

- Can you point to a time when you first encountered the Holy Spirit with a specific effect? If so, describe this.

- Describe your baptism in the Spirit.

- What effect of the Spirit's Presence is most attractive to you? Least attractive? Why?

- Do you consider yourself an "aspiring charismatic"? Why or why not?

RESPOND *to the SPIRIT'S WORK IN YOUR LIFE*

- If you have never received a baptism in the Spirit, why not receive this now?

- If you have already experienced a baptism in the Spirit, why not receive a fresh infilling now?

- What effect do you most desire from your encounter with the Holy Spirit? Ask for that now!

RELATE *to the SPIRIT'S WORK in OTHERS' LIVES*

- Watch Kundayi share his story of powerfully encountering the Holy Spirit on the accompanying DVD.

- Discuss your responses with the small group.

Chapter Four: Help! How Do I Experience You Daily, Holy Spirit?

We can overflow daily with the Spirit—in our work, family, worship, and play. He empowers us to walk and live in His Presence all day long. He teaches us the "unforced rhythms of grace," and His grace flows through us—refreshing others, and us too!

Have you ever stood mesmerized by the beauty of a sparkling mountain stream as it flowed effortlessly over the shiny-smooth rocks, splashing sunlit droplets everywhere? Such a sight takes your breath away. It both refreshes and rests your whole being. That is exactly what the Holy Spirit intends to do in each of our lives. He is the River of Living Water flowing out of our inner man. God desires our lives to have this continual flow of the Spirit's refreshing strength, peace, power, and joy all day long. He wants us to live rested, ready, and refreshed—in the Son. This is not just for church services or special ministry events or an occasional, albeit infrequent, day off. This is not just for days we are well behaved, or we read our Bibles faithfully, or we give in the offering or mow our elderly neighbor's lawn. The Father wants us to live in the continual flow of the Spirit's Presence no matter what we are doing and wherever we are. He wants us to experience the Holy Spirit daily, hourly, even moment by moment, and be energized and encouraged. This is for the best of times and the worst of times!

> He wants us to know and experience the Spirit's delight and help in all of our daily lives—fathering, fighting, winning, losing, cooking, cleaning, pumping gas, and paying our bills.

Busy Lives

But how is this even possible? We live crazy busy lives filled with all kinds of commitments, conversations, and crud that have very little to do with God. Or... do they have *everything* to do with God? As we saw in Chapter 2, God wants to dismantle that dualistic thinking in our lives where we separate our activities into sacred (church stuff—anywhere from one to six hours a week) and secular (all other stuff—maybe 100+ hours a week). He wants us to know and experience the Spirit's delight and help in all of our daily lives—fathering, fighting, winning, losing, cooking, cleaning, pumping gas, and paying our bills.

God loves life here on earth (well, not all the messes, muck, and murders). He created this beautiful earth and designed us, His image-bearing sons and daughters, to tend to the earth and enjoy life. He wants us to raise families, be fulfilled at work, laugh with friends, savor a good glass of wine, make love with our spouse, boogey board in the ocean, and dance to oldies but goodies (okay, I'm a Baby Boomer). God loves life and He loves us! He wants to do life together, in and through us. He loves to play with us, on the field or on the floor. He wants to join us in our work, whether it is wearisome or world-changing, and in our relationships, good and bad. Of course, He loves our worship, too.

He Fills Our Worship

We love Him, because He first loved us. This makes worship easy, and the Holy Spirit fills our worship with His Presence. He flows through us when we gather in a church service with hundreds of others and worship with a full rockin' band, or when we walk outdoors with only Him and hum a chorus with the cardinals (while the trees clap their hands!).

I used to feel guilty as soon as I left church and then enjoyed more hours in the sun than I had spent in church. How foolish of me. I was "in the Son" and He was in me—in or out of church, singing in the pew, or swimming in the pool. It is all good. It is all God. He wants us to experience His Spirit in us as we live life. And trust me, He knows a lot about life. He knows a lot about us.

God Became a Human

God actually became a human being, lived on earth for 33 years, and experienced all the joy and all the sorrow that we humans know. Jesus, 100 percent God, became 100 percent human and accomplished for us what we failed to do ourselves. Jesus, filled with the Holy Spirit, navigated all the suffering, pain, grief, trauma, and darkness that ravaged the world due to sin and Satan. Jesus was tempted in every way any human could be tempted, and yet He remained without sin. Thus, He fulfilled the Law, was sacrificed for our sin, defeated the devil, and rose again to give us a new life—eternal life—in Him.

> Jesus now makes sure we have the Holy Spirit, just as He did, living in union with the Father, helping us live life to the fullest here with that refreshing River of Life always flowing out of us.

Jesus now makes sure we have the Holy Spirit, just as He did, living in union with the Father, helping us live life to the fullest here with that refreshing River of Life always flowing out of us. This is what the Father wants for His children. He loves us and He loves life—the life we live here on earth.

> *And I will ask the Father, and He will give you another Helper to be with you forever... I will not leave you as orphans; I will come to you... In that day you will know that I am in My Father, and you in Me, and I in you (John 14:16, 18, 20 ESV).*

God—Father, Son, and Spirit—lives in us, His children. He wants us to know this for sure and experience the reality now. This is not just some Bible babble.

This is truth. We do not merge with God or become God—that is heresy! But just as the three Persons of the Trinity are distinct, yet one, so are we in our union with God. Confusing? Of course it is. But we do have a Helper who can help us understand it and know it at the level we need to know it. So just pray, "Wow! Help me know that Jesus is in the Father, I am in Jesus, and Jesus is in me. This is almost too good to be true. God lives in me!"

God Wants to Live in and Through Us Here

Our Triune God—Father, Son, and Holy Spirit—lives in dynamic relationship with one another—IN each of us. They bring to our lives both a mind-bending and a beautiful relational oneness. How the God of the Universe fits in "li'l ol' me"—I have no idea. But I know it is true. God longs to flow out of us, bringing His love, joy, peace, and power to our whole lives. Our Creator God created this incredible planet (yes, we've marred it) and human beings in His own image (yes, we've messed up); but He then went to the tremendous cost of redeeming everyone. Was this just so we could all die and go to heaven? No, although we *are* assured of an eternity with Him. But He died and rose again, defeating sin and death, so we could do life here meaningfully, with health and wholeness, love and laughter, power and purpose. And He moved inside of us to make it possible. While this may be a new way of thinking about the Christian life, I want to encourage you to invite the Spirit to make your union with God real to you.

Heaven Only?

One of our dilemmas is we have been taught that what Jesus accomplished in His incarnation only has to do with the hereafter, i.e., getting us fit for heaven; it has little to do with life here, making us fit for heaven to indwell us now. But, the incarnation—God taking on human flesh—is our greatest reason for knowing Truth. The Father loves life here. He has provided the Way for us to have abundant Life now and forever, too. Jesus announced:

> And if I go and prepare a place for you, I will come again and will take you to Myself, that where I am you may be also. And you know the way to where I am going.... I am the Way, and the Truth, and the Life. No one comes to the Father except through Me (John 14:3-4,6 ESV).

Contrary to popular preaching at funerals, Jesus is not talking about building a mansion in heaven and taking us there when we die. No, Jesus is announcing the startling truth that we, like He, can now be one with the Father. This is because Jesus has prepared that place of union for us through His death and resurrection. He is the Way to oneness with God.

Satan, the thief, has tried to steal this radical revelation for centuries!

The thief comes only to steal and kill and destroy. I came that they may have Life and have it abundantly (John 10:10 ESV).

Satan has done a pretty good job of filling our lives with pain and sorrow, guilt and shame. He convinces us that God is only concerned about our "being good enough" to inherit life after death. Satan's voice is often the voice of a pastor, priest, or TV preacher. When we listen to this voice, our lives are cloaked with confusion and condemnation. It's no surprise that many people are tired of trying to live the "Christian" life and turn from faith altogether to eke out some enjoyment here, apart from God. They have no idea that union with God is ours, right now in this life—an abundant life that Jesus gives.

Jesus Invites Us to Live Freely

Jesus knows what religion (and Satan) have done to us, and He invites us to live freely and lightly here. He asks us:

Are you tired? Worn out? Burned out on religion? Come to Me. Get away with Me and you'll recover your life. I'll show you how to take a real rest. Walk with Me and work with Me—watch how I do it. Learn the unforced rhythms of grace. I won't lay anything heavy or ill-fitting on you. Keep company with Me and you'll learn to live freely and lightly (Matthew 11:28-30 MSG).

Really? How inviting! My response: "Yes, Jesus, I would love to walk with You, work with You, watch You, and learn how to live freely and lightly. Are there any requirements or prerequisites to enjoying this adventure with You?"

The only requirements are being tired, worn out, and burned out on religion. That qualifies most of us. Then we simply come to Jesus, who lives in us by His Spirit. We acknowledge His Presence. He assures us that nothing heavy or ill-fitting will be laid on us. He shows us how to take a real rest.

Religion's Lies

Religion has done a bang-up—or should I say "beat-up"—job of squelching our enjoyment as disciples of Jesus. Religion (again, with no thanks to Satan, the liar) perpetrates lies about life: "Life here is not that important and of little interest to God" or "Life is downright disgusting to God." If we don't buy into these lies, we fall for the "If life's not hard here, it's not God" or "If it's the life *you* want, it's not God. Prepare for Siberia!" Religion has robbed us of the truth that God loves His family and wants us to enjoy life here on earth. No wonder we are burned out on religion.

God Loves Life

God is not some uptight, constipated preacher who rails against the glass of wine you sipped at dinner, nor is He clucking His tongue about the time you wasted playing cards with the neighbor. No, He is the God who turned the water into wine (almost the equivalent of 700 bottles!) and thoroughly ticked off the religious stick-in-the muds when He hung out at the despised sinner's (Matthew's) house party. Our God loves life, and He has given us His Spirit to ensure we know how to live it, experiencing Him all day long. Of course, He helps us avoid the excesses and excuses that trip us up in life, but God loves life. This is a lesson we must learn if we are going to experience the Presence of the Holy Spirit all day long.

God Hates Dancing?

In 1965, I was a pimply 14-year-old adolescent with long, skinny legs and an even longer sense of insecurity, intensified by a budding interest in boys. In light of this, it was imperative to me that I enroll in the eighth-grade cotillion dance class, where other pimply teenagers learned to "properly relate" while stumbling over each other's feet with awkward dance moves. It was a rite of passage (at least for the "who's who" of 14-year-olds), and it assured me of an immediate transformation into "cool." However, there was one big problem. My father, in keeping with his religious faith, adamantly refused to give me permission to attend. Dancing, in the eyes of God (and hence my father's eyes), was deemed despicably evil. After my many tears and distraught pleas, my sympathetic mother reluctantly agreed I could go. She reasoned that since the Friday class ended by 5 p.m., I would be back long before my father arrived home from work. All was well until one fateful Friday night when my father stopped by home early, just as I was returning from the dance class. World War III erupted, I was promptly punished, and that was the last dance for me.

This incident, along with many others, slowly but surely convinced me that God hated good times. Whether it was the intense excitement of a crosstown rival basketball game, a premier showing of *Doctor Zhivago,* or the mere purchase of *Rubber Soul,* the Beatles' latest album, I knew God was disgusted with all of it and quite repulsed by my participation in any of it. It has been a long healing journey to finally be convinced otherwise.

God Delights in So Much

Thanks to the relentless love and desire of the Holy Spirit, I finally came to believe that God actually delights in sports, music, theater, dance, and art. What brilliant color these pursuits add to life! You might ask, "But can't these be idolized, abused, or perverted?" Of course they can. So can food, drink, work, sex, and shopping! That's again why the Holy Spirit is so necessary in our lives. He teaches us to delight in, not to depend on, these activities.

> Freedom comes through the power of the Holy Spirit living inside of us, whether it is freedom from religion or freedom from reckless living. We want to live Spirit-led lives, not sinful, selfish ones.

Freedom

Some of you, unlike me, have no experience with the stranglehold of legalistic, fun-robbing religion. However, you may have been ensnared by the pleasures of the world to the extent you are addicted or in bondage. Freedom comes through the power of the Holy Spirit living inside of us, whether it is freedom from religion or freedom from reckless living. We want to live Spirit-led lives, not sinful, selfish ones. This can be a slow, painful lesson. But trust me, we can trust Him! That's why His gift of the Holy Spirit, the Teacher, is so valuable to teach us the "unforced rhythms of grace" that Jesus talked about. These are an important bridge to living freely and lightly.

Unforced Rhythms of Grace

The unforced rhythms of grace allow and equip us to enjoy a life flowing with that River of the Spirit—a life filled with righteousness, peace, and joy.

The Holy Spirit teaches us how to exercise these unforced rhythms of grace. These are what are commonly known as spiritual disciplines—practices like Bible reading, praying, journaling, and worshiping are important ways for us to connect and communicate with God. They are neither rigid nor forced. They are not boring "quiet times." They are rhythms of *grace*—God's empowering influence on our lives—and they flow out of our love relationship with Him. They teach us a new way to live.

New Habits Needed

As we learned in Chapter 2, we have brand new hearts—heart transplants from God—and we need to learn new habits, new thoughts, and a new way of life. Sometimes our minds and even our lives are still filled with junk, and we need help. The old life has to go. We cannot live two lives! Paul instructs us:

> *And so I insist—and God backs me up on this—that there be no going along with the crowd, the empty-headed, mindless crowd... Feeling no pain, they let themselves go in sexual obsession, addicted to every sort of perversion. But that's no life for you. You learned Christ! My assumption is that you have paid careful attention to Him, been well instructed in the truth precisely as we have it in Jesus.*
>
> *Since, then, we do not have the excuse of ignorance, everything—and I do mean everything—connected with that old way of life has to go. It's rotten through and through. Get rid of it! And then take on an entirely new way of life—a God-fashioned life, a life renewed from the inside and working itself into your conduct as God accurately reproduces His character in you (Ephesians 4:17-24 MSG).*

We learned Christ! We now have new lives in Jesus and Jesus in us. We have brand new natures. The "old me" is dead, and with it went that rotten way of life into the grave. We are renewed from the inside. We may not always feel this, but the Holy Spirit helps bring this transformation. He is our personal trainer. Training (spiritual or physical) takes time and commitment. The training empowers us to live free from our old, rotten lives and grow in our new, healthy lives. We are no longer just "sinners saved by grace." We are now "saints strengthened by grace." Whoopee!

Set Aside a Specific Time for "Training"

To experience the Spirit daily, set aside specific time to focus on your relationship with Him, using several of these rhythms or practices. This is just as in any healthy relationship, where we set aside time to have lighthearted walks, serious talks, or special times of making love. This is essential to a wholesome relationship. And like the union of marriage, where we are one from the moment we say "I do," we are one with Jesus from the moment we are born again. We don't do these practices to "get closer" to Jesus or to ascend some "ladder to oneness," just as we don't do things to be "more married" (although we can do lots of things to have more enjoyable marriages!). We are already one with God, just as Jesus reminded us in His prayer to the Father:

> *The glory that You have given Me I have given to them, that they may be ONE even as We are ONE, I in them and You in Me, that they may become perfectly ONE, so that the world may know that You sent Me and loved them even as You loved Me (John 17:22-23 ESV, emphasis mine).*

We are one—in real union—with the God who loves us as much as He loves Jesus. By His grace, we are already righteous, loved, and redeemed sons and daughters.

Trying Hard Does Not Work

For years, I read the ancient mystics and tried hard to follow their step-by-step instructions to achieving intimate union with God. I saw this truth in the Scriptures. I knew union with God was mine. But I fasted, prayed, meditated, kept quiet, sang loud—all to no avail. I couldn't seem to get any closer to Jesus. I tried to imitate Him and then ask if that was good enough to achieve intimacy. I only grew more discouraged. Then I discovered (thank you, Holy Spirit!) I was as close to Jesus as I was going to ever get—I was *already* in union with God. I was one with God, just like Jesus said. Jesus had done all the hard work to make it possible. Did I really think my work could do a better job than His work? I needed to trust Him and His work, not trust me and my work.

> We do not strive FOR acceptance and approval from the Father. We grow FROM a secure place of acceptance and approval from God. We do not try to imitate Jesus. We learn to be intimate with Him who lives in us by His Spirit.

We Grow FROM, not FOR

We grow into the fullness of who we already are as new people in Christ. We do not strive FOR acceptance and approval from the Father. We grow FROM a secure place of acceptance and approval from God. We do not try to imitate Jesus. We learn to be intimate with Him who lives in us by His Spirit. Our growth is enhanced as we engage in these rhythms. They enable us to take a real rest—the rest of faith—as we learn to live freely and lightly in union with the Father, Son, and Spirit.

"Jesus, are You in me?"

I like what author and theologian C. Baxter Kruger encourages us to do every morning. He says, "As soon as you wake up, be still and ask, 'Jesus, are You in me?' and then wait until you are aware of His Presence." Jesus has not left us overnight while we slept, but we can lose awareness of Him. We can feel alone in those dark, early morning moments.

Tomorrow morning, ask: "Jesus are You in me?" This is a great way to start the day and to "keep company" with Jesus.

Choose What You Like to Do

We choose when and how we will spend personal "training" time with the Holy Spirit. Some people prefer mornings, others like night the best. Some love indoors by the fire, others choose outdoors in the forest. The important thing: do choose a consistent time and place.

Engage in those practices that are most beneficial for *your* relationship with God. Some of us love to meditate on the Bible, others prefer worship music, while others pray the Psalms or write in journals or read devotionals. Each person discovers what works best. Many great resources can help us. Check out the Resources page.

Hearing God's Voice

Through all of this training, we learn to hear God's voice more clearly. This is often a fresh thought popping in our minds that gives us help for a specific challenge, or it may be just a word of encouragement. It sounds similar to your own voice, yet it is distinct. We grow familiar with it as we do with the voices of those we know and love.

And there are times when God's voice sounds quite distinct from our voice, too, and we are ensured that it is Him. For example, Tom, a member of our Vineyard church, one day found himself battling an array of significant neurological symptoms that came upon him both swiftly and severely (and worsened over a few months before he was miraculously healed). In his words: "I was fine one moment, and felt like I was hurtling headlong into darkness the next. That first evening, as I was grappling with what was going on, and fighting off—not very well, I might add!—panic and fear, I clearly heard, amidst all the clamor and chaos, a very calm voice in my head that surely wasn't mine: *This is a spiritual battle, and the battle is Mine.*" Tom relates that he was not only physically healed—on the day a word was given at church that God was healing someone with neurological problems—but that he experienced a life-altering spiritual healing that was even more significant. And he knew that "still, small voice" was God's, because it was so foreign to what he was thinking.

Of course, we make mistakes and don't always hear perfectly, but our Father would rather we take baby steps, fall, and get back up, than not take any steps at all. He is always there, ready to help us hear more clearly. He loves us. He does not chide us for our missteps. Nor does He micromanage our lives with robotic-like instructions: "Eat this, go there, say that." We live in union with God. This is a beautiful friendship, not a master-slave ownership.

Beware of Misunderstanding

There is so much misunderstanding about the spiritual practices or rhythms. They are unforced, done willingly with God's gracious help. These practices are not to gain favor with God. We already have undeserved favor— grace—that is ours based on Jesus, not on us. If we never, ever read the Bible again, went to church, gave money, prayed, served others—God still loves us furiously. God's love is based on what Jesus has done for us, not on what we do for Him.

Rhythms Help Us Love

So why bother committing to these practices? Because rhythms of grace help us love God more—as we read His Word, talk with Him, obey Him, love Him. We put ourselves in a place to grow in God's grace. His grace flows to us and through us. We are opening up to His channels of grace, and in doing so, we are strengthened. We are healthy and able to overcome tough obstacles. These practices help us live victoriously over the evil one and experience the Holy Spirit daily, flowing in and through us like that pure sparkling stream.

We are Weak, But He is Strong

Interestingly, we live in this strange awareness of how weak we are and how strong He is. This is Kingdom Life. This is not an internal conflict between a bad heart and good heart. This is not the devil on one shoulder and an angel on the other, both trying to influence us. There are not two dogs fighting inside of us. These are all crazy illustrations in Christian literature that proclaim to be a picture of our lives as believers.

Jesus lives IN us. When we encounter difficult stuff throughout our day, we can feel like we are failing or we are sinful or unacceptable to God. We may doubt that we have new hearts or that the Spirit is in us. But the Spirit, our Helper, freely imparts His grace, His strength, His wisdom, His life, and His power to us on a moment-to-moment basis.

When you encounter difficulties, stop! Remember He is in you, and wait until you are aware of Him. He enables you to live freely and lightly with nothing heavy weighing on you all day long.

Is this possible? Yes, even at our work—where it is often needed most!

God Designed You for Your Work

Fon is a brilliant, world-famous mechanical engineering professor at the University of Illinois who works long hours and travels the globe sharing his expertise. He is a warm, engaging man who loves his students and listens to and thoughtfully answers their questions about the design and operation of powerful machines. He is also always ready to answer their many questions about the design and operation of his God, who they see reflected in his lifestyle but who is a distant or nonexistent deity to many of them. Fon understands that God gifted him to teach this complicated subject, and he honors God by relying fully on the Holy Spirit to lead him and help him. He experiences the Spirit daily in his work, although he may never do any sort of formal Bible study in his office.

Sadly, many do not know what Fon knows: God designed him especially for this work and loves to help him be the best at his job. It is common for people to separate their daily work, careers, and ordinary tasks from the Presence of God. It is not intentional, per se. It just never crosses their minds that God is all that interested in their work or wants to be involved. But this is not true.

> God loves work and He is so ready to help you by His Spirit, giving you fresh ideas, energy, and purpose in your work. You can experience the Holy Spirit all day long at work, and I do not mean because you try to do spiritual things on your lunch hour like read your Bible or pray with a coworker.

God loves work and He is so ready to help you by His Spirit, giving you fresh ideas, energy, and purpose in your work. You can experience the Holy Spirit all day long at work, and I do not mean because you try to do spiritual things on your lunch hour like read your Bible or pray with a coworker. You can do that, too, but God loves your work.

God Has Great Ideas for Us

God is so smart and has lots of great ideas, inventions, and strategies to reveal to those who ask. He wants us to be the best at our jobs, to work at jobs we actually enjoy and were designed for. As we learn how to better listen for and hear His voice, we will partner with God together in our work. God doesn't "need" teachers, farmers, scientists, doctors, truck drivers, or computer whizzes. He could do all of that work on His own, thank you very much! But, how glorious that He loves to partner with us in our work.

Partnering with the Spirit to Help Others

My brother, Tim Hoerr, CEO of Serra Ventures, has had an exciting adventure partnering with the Holy Spirit in his work. He shares this story:

We operate a micro-venture fund that reviews hundreds of investment opportunities per year and selects about 10 of them for our portfolio. Our portfolio focuses on early stage, high technology enterprises. I initially met Brett and Ross, the cofounders of Nanomedical Diagnostics, in June, 2014. They had recently formed the company around a unique graphene sensor technology that showed real promise for very early detection of Lyme Disease.

Lyme Disease affects 30,000 people in the US every year, and many tens of thousands of others worldwide. It is particularly difficult to detect, often taking weeks or months for the symptoms to fully manifest. And, unfortunately, the later the symptoms manifest, the more difficult Lyme Disease is to treat. It can be a highly debilitating disease, often lasting years in terms of its impact.

I maintained contact with the company over the course of 2014, receiving periodic updates. And then in December of 2014, I arranged for another on-site visit with Ross and Brett. I had a great conversation with the cofounders that day. The company met most of our stringent criteria for investment—yet I wasn't completely sure if we should proceed. Early-stage companies can be particularly difficult to evaluate, and whether they will ultimately be successful is impossible to tell. Making the investment decision is always a calculated risk. After leaving the meeting that afternoon, I asked the Holy Spirit to give me clarity of direction regarding a potential investment in the company. While I had a positive overall feeling about doing the deal, I really desired to receive confirmation from the Spirit that Serra Ventures should proceed.

Later than evening, my wife and I attended a neighborhood potluck dinner. We sat next to a couple we didn't know, learning soon that they were visiting from Toronto. About five minutes into the conversation, unprompted, they began telling us the story of their adult daughter who was suffering from Lyme Disease. They painstakingly related her three-year journey of a late diagnosis of Lyme, followed by months of antibody therapy that had limited effectiveness. It was a heart-wrenching story.

Up to that point in my life, I had never spoken with anyone about Lyme Disease in general, let alone in such personal detail. In the mid-

dle of the conversation with this couple, I knew that the Holy Spirit was confirming to me the enormity of this problem and that we were to take the risk and invest in this company.

Flash forward to 2017—the company has made tremendous progress; they are currently selling a version of their instrument suitable for research purposes, while preparing for future FDA approval; they have struck a partnership with Mayo Clinic that is the number one processing center for Lyme Disease diagnosis in the US; they are also working with the US Centers for Disease Control and Prevention to test their instrument for both Lyme and Zika. It is quite an adventure to work with the Holy Spirit. He has help for real problems!

Help for Difficult Times at Work

"I wanted to strangle her," hissed Janelle through clenched teeth. "I could not believe she was showing up for the staff meeting 15 minutes late... again! This was the third time in one month. Although angry, I dreaded the difficult conversation ahead of me. Help, Holy Spirit!"

The Holy Spirit is great at helping us with difficult conversations and decisions that most of us encounter in our workplace. Next time you face a difficult situation, just softly welcome the Holy Spirit to fill you with all you need to navigate it well and not succumb to selfishness (such as giving into your anger). Choose to walk in the Spirit and not according to feelings:

My counsel is this: Live freely, animated and motivated by God's Spirit. Then you won't feed the compulsions of selfishness....These two ways of life are antithetical, so that you cannot live at times one way and at times another way according to how you feel on any given day. Why don't you choose to be led by the Spirit...? (Galatians 5:6-18 MSG).

We can make a choice: be led by the Spirit who lives inside of us. He releases help for daily difficulties. Janelle was empowered to have the difficult conversation with her tardy staff member. With the Spirit's help, she patiently listened first (instead of flying off the handle) and discovered the woman had childcare problems that caused her to be late. Together, they forged an amiable solution. She is learning to live freely, animated by the Spirit.

The Spirit at Work

I love how my friend Debbie has beautifully walked with the Holy Spirit in her job as a nurse practitioner. Women wait to get an appointment with her because she truly cares about their concerns and has sound medical advice. And, yes, she freely prays with her patients if they so desire, but this is not the only way the Spirit is active in her work. She genuinely loves people and lets the River of Life in her flow out as she takes their blood pressure or counsels them through a difficult diagnosis. Just tuning in to the Spirit's presence in her helps her handle the stress of a busy medical practice. She gets to experience the Spirit daily, and not just wait until she goes to church or is alone with her Bible study material. She partners with the Spirit at work.

> I do not head to work without first asking the Spirit to help me with all the challenges I will face that day. His wisdom, strength, patience, and humor are imperative for a successful workday. Don't leave home "without Him"! Oh, wait, we are His home—even at work!

You've no doubt heard of the annual "Take Your Child to Work Day." Well, *every* day for us is "Take the Holy Spirit to Work Day"! I do not head to work without first asking the Spirit to help me with all the challenges I will face that day. His wisdom, strength, patience, and humor are imperative for a successful workday. Don't leave home without Him! Oh, wait, we *are* His home—even at work!

Be an Example at Work—Both Ethical and Enjoyable!

Carl had the mistaken notion that partnering with God in his work just meant he was diligent to make ethical decisions and uphold a high moral code of conduct on the job. While he was a great example of this, he tended to be a bit uptight about everything—even going overboard at times to make sure he paid the extra quarter if he refilled his half-empty coffee cup, sometimes clucking at those who didn't. Nothing wrong with being ethical (actually, everything *right* about being ethical!), but we can cross a line of flaunting this to our fellow workers. Yes, we are sent to reflect the character of Jesus, who lives inside us. It goes without saying—I hope, but I'll say it anyway—that we should live morally, on and off the job. However, this does not mean we police others or present a "holier than thou" attitude. On the other hand, we work in a manner that influences others by our choices, example, and joyful attitudes—all made possible by the Holy Spirit within.

I love how J Leman, a former college and NFL football player (and my own son!) did exactly that. On the teams he played on, J worked among a messy, mixed bag of immorality, violence, disrespect, profanity, and promiscuity. Yet, he was a very popular player with his teammates and coaches, despite his different lifestyle. He refused to look down on or criticize others, but he did not join in their junk either. He lived and played with a "secret weapon" inside him—the Holy Spirit. A River of Life flowed out of him and splashed all over his coworkers. Some actually enjoyed the "Spirit shower"!

Jesus loves to be present in our work. He, of course, worked many years as a carpenter—many times longer than He did in actual ministry. He sees much worth in our work, and He wants us to be fulfilled in our chosen careers.

Invite His Spirit to give you new perspective, purpose, and power in your work. I love the perspective of my friend, Alan Scott who is pastor of the Colerarine, Ireland Vineyard Church. When asked how many ministers he has at the church, he responds, "Oh, about 2,000—all over this city!" Yes! All of us are ministers, wherever we go, whatever we do. The Holy Spirit flows through us. Ask Him to show you what a unique, one-of-a-kind person you are. Ask Him what He has deposited in you for you to give away at this time and place in history. You might be surprised!

You Are Unique

The Father loves showing us how unique, special, and wonderful we each are to Him. We are indeed His workmanship, a real work of art by our Creator, and He has a specific destiny for each of us.

If you were raised in a strict religious home or church as I was, then you may struggle with CCS—Christian Clone Syndrome. This is a prevalent problem in many church circles that demands all look alike, act alike, think alike, and adjust their personalities to fit the group and its rules. I truly suffered from this, and I did not fit the religious mode for women in my church family. Women were not allowed to speak at all in church gatherings (not even give out hymn numbers), and I knew from a fairly early age that I loved to speak in public, on stage, and not just to other women. I would later discover I was actually called to preach—another absolute no-no in my religious system (and in many others, even today!). I tried valiantly to be a good Christian clone, and was absolutely miserable and ultimately rebellious, finally culminating in my being found and filled by the Holy Spirit.

> He reminds us over and over how pleasing each of us is to the Father who created us, and who gave each of us the personality and gifting that He did. The Spirit reminds us that we will never walk in the fullness of joy until we say yes to all He has made each of us to be.

The Holy Spirit Shows Us

The Holy Spirit wants you to shout: Jesus loves ME. Jesus LOVES me. JESUS loves me. He reminds us over and over how pleasing each of us is to the Father who created us, and who gave each of us the personality and gifting that He did. The Spirit reminds us that we will never walk in the fullness of joy until we say *yes* to all He has made each of us to be. This is so freeing. We no longer have to compare or compete with others. We are one of a kind. And we are deeply loved. We are in union with Him, but we do not lose our own personalities in that oneness. We become neither a groupie nor a "god." Thank God! Each one of us can discover who we are, embrace our destinies, and change the world with Jesus. But, beware of anxiety. This can disrupt and derail us—daily!

Freedom from Anxiety

We live in anxious, tumultuous times. A brief glance at the news feed is enough to stir real fear. But the Spirit wants us to live free from worry, fear, and anxiety. Jesus reminds us of this over and over:

> *Therefore I tell you, do not be anxious about your life, what you will eat or what you will drink, nor about your body, what you will put on. Is not life more than food, and the body more than clothing? (Matthew 6:25 ESV).*

It is hard not to worry about daily life, but if we want to have that River of Life flowing out of us, we can't be consumed with daily anxiety. It debilitates us. It affects our work. The Holy Spirit taught me a valuable lesson while

I was in the throes of a difficult job—motherhood—but this applies to any job! The lesson: don't worry, be happy, and pray—just like Paul wrote:

Always be full of joy in the Lord.... Don't worry about anything; instead, pray about everything. Tell God what you need, and thank Him for all He has done. Then you will experience God's peace, which exceeds anything we can understand. His peace will guard your hearts and minds as you live in Christ Jesus (Philippians 4: 4a, 6-7 TLB).

I wanted that peace. I wanted to be free of the dark cloud of depression that descended without warning. I wanted my heart and mind to be protected as I tried to *"live in Christ Jesus."* But I only had a few quiet moments alone with Jesus every day. I was the mother of five rambunctious children, ranging from newborn to 10 years old. My days were filled with endless activities and sometimes trivial but overwhelming challenges. I was often changing a diaper, pushing a swing at the park, nursing a high fever, reading *Mike Mulligan,* or building a fort with blankets and a card table—all in between cooking, cleaning, and carting to and fro. In addition, I was home-schooling the older children, sorting mounds of dirty laundry—with lessons on measurement thrown in for good measure (no pun intended). Sure, nap-time was a brief respite, but by then, I usually fell fast asleep, too. Not only was I in the mess and stress of raising a bunch of kids, but my husband and I were also trying to pastor a growing, messy, church. And so, in my harried state, if I found my mind was free for more than five seconds, I sometimes muttered a hurried prayer: "Help, Holy Spirit! How can I worry about nothing and pray about everything and live in Christ Jesus all day long? I want, I need peace!"

Practicing the Presence

Then, I "stumbled" across a book (Holy Spirit stumble!) called *Practicing the Presence of God.* A monk, Brother Lawrence, who lived in the 1600s, wrote this book. He was a crippled man who worked in a monastery kitch-en, a job he actually hated. But he determined to live every moment acutely aware of God's loving, empowering Presence in him. He actively surren-dered to God's Presence moment by moment. He talked with Jesus about his needs and thanked Him for His provisions and told Jesus how much he loved Him. The results?

Brother Lawrence had a life of peace, joy, and delight, no matter the circumstance, for 40 years. He had the River of Life flowing out of him, and others took notice. Thankfully, he wrote letters detailing how he engaged in practicing the Presence of God, because so many people wanted to know his secret to such a happy life. Those letters, written over 400 years ago, became the book—a book that changed me and millions of others through the centuries.

Lessons Learned

This book, along with the Holy Spirit, taught me how to talk with God in such a way that I never again had to be consumed with fear, anxiety, or depression. I didn't say I wasn't given the opportunity over and over, and I have to confess that I failed many times. During a busy day, it was so easy to forget. But all throughout the day, in ordinary events and happenings like eating, showering, cleaning, sitting at my computer, driving my car, meeting with others, or caring for kids, I simply chose to be aware of and enjoy Jesus living in me.

> The Spirit would gently remind me again that He never leaves and is right inside, waiting to help. I learned through many struggles to practice the Presence of Jesus and enjoy the amazing benefits of the Holy Spirit all day long.

He wanted to handle all my worries and fears. I sometimes lived as a "functional atheist," as though God did not exist. I thought I could handle my own life, thank you very much, but was soon overcome by anxiety, fear, and depression. The Spirit would gently remind me again that He never leaves and is right inside, waiting to help. I learned through many struggles to practice the Presence of Jesus and enjoy the amazing benefits of the Holy Spirit all day long. I learned to rejoice, not worry. I learned to pray and tell God what I needed. I learned to remember to thank Him for all His provision, which I so routinely forgot to do.

He Will Never Leave

He has promised to never leave us, no matter the circumstance, our condition, situation, or sinful action. He does not come and go. It can seem that way at times. He can seem a long way off. But Jesus never leaves. We may obscure His presence by our attitudes or our sin. We may doubt His presence because we are relying on our feelings. We may be confused by the lies of the enemy. We may "hide" from Him in guilt or shame. But through it all He is there, right inside of us, waiting to reconnect and remind us of His love.

Son Conscious, Not Sin Conscious

Sometimes, we have to recall that His work, and not our own work, is what already cleansed us from all unrighteousness, from all sin. The Spirit reminds us over and over, because the enemy's voice speaks condemnation and shame. We choose to stay "Son Conscious" and not "Sin Conscious," except to confess again that we believe He has taken our sins away, made us new, and lives inside of us.

Peace Like a River

The Spirit wants to release His peace to flood over our lives—peace like a river. Practicing His Presence is a powerful tool for this to happen. When we choose to recall moment-by-moment that Jesus is really in us with His loving, empowering Spirit, and we choose to practice His Presence, and surrender to the reality of this Presence, we are flooded with His peace and joy. We can more easily hear His voice that instructs or assures us. We have a conversation with Him. We talk with our invisible God whose peace is made visible in our lives.

Practicing His Presence does not mean the actual circumstances will always change, but sometimes they do. A mistake I made early on when practicing this was I thought by tuning into the Presence of Jesus in me, then the sickness would leave or the tire would not be flat anymore or the baby would stop crying. Not necessarily. Instead, we choose to surrender to His Presence in us. He fills us with Jesus's peace, wisdom, and patience—fruits of the Spirit.

Abiding Bears Fruit

When we Practice His Presence, we choose to be alert and aware, and to believe every moment that Jesus is in us and loves us. While this is not automatic, it does get easier, more habitual and natural. We are confident of His pleasure in all aspects of our life. We simply set our minds to remember, and then we watch Him bear the fruit of the Spirit in us.

This is exactly what Jesus said our relationship with Him would look like when He compared it to a vine and a branch, with abundant fruit:

> *Abide in Me, and I in you. As the branch cannot bear fruit by itself, unless it abides in the vine, neither can you, unless you abide in Me. I am the vine; you are the branches. Whoever abides in Me and I in him, he it is that bears much fruit, for apart from Me you can do nothing (John 15:4-5 ESV).*

Abide means to "take up permanent residence in." We are attached to Jesus like a branch is to a vine—one with the vine—life flowing from one to the other. We live, dwell, and rest in Him. We are not apart from Him. This union is so freeing and so fruitful, too. This is the Bride (me) and her Groom (Jesus) living in oneness and fruitfulness. This is not just a "faith fact"—it is real, tangible, and alive. Here are the results:

> *But what happens when we live God's way? He brings gifts into our lives, much the same way that fruit appears in an orchard—things like affection for others, exuberance about life, serenity. We develop a willingness to stick with things, a sense of compassion in the heart, and a conviction that a basic holiness permeates things and people. We find ourselves involved in loyal commitments, not needing to force our way in life, able to marshal and direct our energies wisely (Galatians 5:22-23 MSG).*

Yes! This is a life of fruitfulness, and it starts with faith—faith of the Son of God, who loved us, gave His life for us, and moved right in. The Spirit is inside us, bringing out the very best. The Spirit is releasing faith in us, because Jesus is the author of that faith—the faith of God. When we do encounter situations or circumstances that trigger fear, worry, or concern of any kind, we can simply talk with Jesus and ask Him for what we need, and trust Him for the answers.

Stop Living in the Past and Future

Many of us do not actually live in the present, so it is very difficult to practice His Presence. Oh, sure, we are in the present, but our minds are occupied with the past or future. We are dwelling on: "If only I hadn't said that... or eaten two donuts... or bought the new phone..." or "What if I fail the test... or lose my job... or get sick...." We live in the past or future. Regret and worry bloat our minds and drain our lives of peace.

Live in the Now

It is especially important to live in the now and not in the future. Author William Paul Young calls living in the future, "future tripping." He suggests the brilliant (and might I add, Biblical!) idea that we "live in the grace of one day." It is tempting to live in the future, planning the day away, anticipating some upcoming event, worrying about some possible problem, and totally miss out on living in the Presence in the present. We end up wasting today's grace on tomorrow's problems—most of which never happen! Someone much smarter than I said:

> *That is why I tell you not to worry about everyday life—whether you have enough food and drink, or enough clothes to wear. Isn't life more than food, and your body more than clothing...? Can all your worries add a single moment to your life?... And if God cares so wonderfully for wildflowers that are here today and thrown into the fire tomorrow, He will certainly care for you. Why do you have so little faith? (Matthew 6:25,27,30 NLT).*

I agree with Jesus! We can trust God to care for us today, tomorrow, and forever.

"Enjoy the present in His Presence." I say this phrase out loud to remind myself throughout the day, especially when I get distracted. I want to live in the grace for today. It is always enough.

Enjoy the Present in His Presence

"Enjoy the present in His Presence." I say this phrase out loud to remind myself throughout the day, especially when I get distracted. I want to live in the grace for today. It is always enough. As a matter of fact, it is grace upon grace—abounding grace, abundant grace (Romans 5:17, 20)—truly amazing grace.

Thank you, Holy Spirit, for filling us to overflowing with this River of Life—at work, at play, and in worship. Thank you for being our personal trainer, empowering us to face each day with Your love, joy, peace, and strength. Thank you for never leaving us in the lurch, for always being present to take our worries and fill us with Your peace. Doing life with You is fun and fruitful, too. We love you, Holy Spirit!

REFLECT *on the SPIRIT'S WORK IN YOUR LIFE*

- Where do you struggle the most to experience the Spirit's Presence—work, play, worship? Explain.

- Which "rhythms" work best for you to be trained by the Spirit?

- Share how you spend alone time with the Spirit.

- What is your experience with "future tripping"?

RESPOND *to the SPIRIT'S WORK in YOUR LIFE*

- What changes can you make right now to daily experience the Holy Spirit?

- What is a new rhythm you could practice with the Spirit to grow in your new life?

- How might the Spirit be more involved in your work?

- How might you live in the "grace for one day"?

RELATE *to the SPIRIT'S WORK in OTHER'S LIVES*

- Watch Danelle share her story of daily experiencing the Holy Spirit on the accompanying DVD.

- Discuss your responses with the small group.

HELLO
HOLY
SPIRIT

Chapter Five:
Help! How Do I
Trust You in Tough
Times, Holy Spirit?

*The Holy Spirit works powerfully in our tough situations—
tragedies, temptations, and everyday troubles.
He strengthens us, comforts us, and even prays for us
and through us. He shows us God is very good, we are
deeply loved, and we can fully trust Jesus.*

"I don't know why God gave my child leukemia," the young mother sobbed. "I guess He knew I needed to grow stronger in my faith, but I am really struggling. Is God good? Does He really care? I am so confused." Of course she is struggling. Of course she is confused.

If you have a child suffering with cancer, your world crashes. And when you also believe that God *caused* your child's cancer, you and your faith are decimated. This is tragic on all fronts and it need not be.

God Does Not Send Tragedy

The belief that God causes trouble and tragedy is 100 percent false. Our loving Father, who gave His only Son to take our sorrow and pain, is not a schizophrenic God who afflicts our children with cancer. Nothing could be further from the truth. Yet this belief is preached from pulpits around the world, and it is often the impetus for people's ultimate rejection of God.

Satan Destroys Humans; Jesus Destroys Him

Fathers on earth who burn or beat their children to "teach them a lesson" are arrested and imprisoned. How twisted to think our heavenly Father would commit such a crime. We know the enemy is Satan, the father of lies, and he has a long record of killing and destroying. We also know that through Jesus's death and resurrection, He defeated Satan, destroyed his works, and now has all authority over him. This truth is the foundation for trusting God in tough times. We can trust a good God.

Tension of Two Kingdoms

Tough times come to us because we still live in the tension of two kingdoms here on earth—God's Kingdom of Light and Satan's kingdom of darkness. We may experience the tragic loss of a young child, the dreaded diagnosis of a terminal disease, a devastating divorce, or a deadly accident. These are very serious troubles. But it is just as serious to attribute these to God. These tragedies belong to the kingdom of darkness. Our good Father does not cause these.

Jesus Shows Us the Father

Jesus, the exact reflection of the Father, showed us what the Father is like and what the Father does. Jesus raised a 12-year-old girl from death, healed an epileptic boy of demons, forgave an adulterous woman and a crooked businessman, calmed a storm that threatened the life of His disciples, and gave sight to a man born blind—to name just a few of His everyday activities. Over and over, He showed us God is the giver of only good gifts, and God our Father does not change:

So don't be misled, my dear brothers and sisters. Whatever is good and perfect is a gift coming down to us from God our Father, who created all the lights in the heavens. He never changes or casts a shifting shadow (James 1:16-17 NLT).

> Please do not acquiesce to patronizing sentiments that pontificate how cancer, death, disappointment, and tragedy are somehow "gifts" from God. That is patently false! Our God never changes or casts a shifting shadow. He created all the lights in the heavens and He Himself is 100 percent Light. There is no darkness in Him.

Please do not acquiesce to patronizing sentiments that pontificate how cancer, death, disappointment, and tragedy are somehow "gifts" from God. That is patently false! Our God never changes or casts a shifting shadow. He created all the lights in the heavens and He Himself is 100 percent Light. There is no darkness in Him.

God Does Good

Does God take our tough times and turn them into good? Of course! He is our Healer, our Savior. But, be sure of this: He is not a sadist. He is not an afflicter. He is not two-faced. God is good—all the time—and He goes about doing good:

> *And you know that God anointed Jesus of Nazareth with the Holy Spirit and with power. Then Jesus went around doing good and healing all who were oppressed by the devil, for God was with Him (Acts 10:38 NLT).*

The devil is the oppressor. God is the Deliverer. The Holy Spirit brings freedom. Thank God! We can trust Him.

Trouble is in the World

While the big troubles really knock us out, we also deal with much smaller, yet annoying trials: an inconvenient flat tire, a whining kid, a surprise D on an essay, or a nasty neighbor. Troubles—big and small—are here for all. Jesus reminds us:

> *I have said these things to you, that in Me you may have peace. In the world you will have tribulation. But take heart; I have overcome the world (John 16:33 ESV).*

Yes, all around us there are troubles, but we can have peace in Jesus because He has overcome the world; He has defeated Satan, and He lets us in on that victory. He wants us to take heart, be joyful, and trust Him in tough times. Remember, we are in Him and He is in us. He is a master at taking our pain and releasing His peace. And yes, I hear your question (and mine!): "But how does He do this in real life—my life?"

It is always a matter of simple faith—believing God is truly good, lives inside of you, loves you, and helps you. There are no complicated hoops to jump through. Believe and receive His help. Trust the Helper in you. His love never fails.

A Fatal Ride

He was a handsome, budding athlete, full of life and vigor, with the typical 14-year-old swagger. His one last fling with friends—before high school began the next day—was a joyride in the country on a steamy August afternoon. Except, he never made it to high school the next day or ever. He died that night in the ER from multiple injuries suffered when the 100-mph joyride turned fatal. I stood with his parents at the hospital, crying out to God, hoping for a miracle. That did not happen. As the shock of his death registered, grief gushed forth and consumed us.

Grief

You can't control grief. You can't tame grief. Grief wraps you in its inescapable tentacles and squeezes you until you gasp for breath, choke on your tears, and collapse, inconsolable.

Grief is one of the most painful of all emotions because it always emanates from some tragedy, death, or loss. We need comfort beyond human hugs and weak words. We need heavenly help.

The Comforter

The Holy Spirit, the Comforter, lives in us. He does not take a holiday or go into hiding when grief barges in with its destructive pain and sets up residence. We can trust the Spirit to deal with this unwanted and unwieldy trespasser. The Holy Spirit navigates through the deep crevices of our pain, fills them with His healing oil, and comforts us. But we do need to choose to trust Him, and this can be difficult when our feelings overwhelm us. Comfort does come, but we may need the Spirit to show us how He camps inside our grief and cries with us, releasing knots of pain. Then, His Presence comforts us with the ability to not ask "why," but to rest in His love.

Sharing Healing

My friends tasted the Spirit's comfort and eventually were nourished and strengthened enough to start a support group called Griefshare. Here they shared the Spirit's comfort and healing with others who had suffered loss. Community is so important when we experience tough times. We share one another's burdens, and this lightens the load of our wounded heart.

"Time heals all wounds," the old adage proclaims. Really? While time can help to heal, the Spirit, our Helper, truly does heal. Our Helper heals all wounds. And He is ready at all times, even when we least expect to need Him.

Friend or Foe?

Friendships have never been easy for me, even though I am an outgoing, conversational person and I am at ease with large groups at my dinner table. In my work as a pastor, I am committed to carrying many others' personal confidences in my heart, so I keep quiet. I also tend to keep my own concerns and cares in my heart, shared only with God (who already knows anyway). My hesitancy to share means I have just a few close friends with whom I "pour"—pour an intimate cup of coffee, pour out my heart, and pour forth painful tears without restraint. Jane (not her real name) was such a friend, and I treasured our special bond of love. We nurtured this bond by sharing. We shared deep secrets and difficult dilemmas. On a lighter note, we shared delicious recipes and favorite movies. We trusted each other whether we were doing Bible study or decorating my family room. Ours was a "match made in heaven." This was so rare for me and yet so safe and satisfying. Thus, to say that I was "surprised" or merely "saddened" can't begin to describe the extreme shock I experienced when one day, out of the blue, Jane announced that she and her family were leaving our church, where I pastor, to attend a "more proper" denomination in our city. Our friendship was over, she sheepishly confessed. Our bond was broken. It wouldn't work to remain friends.

My heart was shattered. My secrets were exposed. My fears realized. What a fool I had been! My friend had become my foe. If you have never been the shepherd of a flock of people, you may not get why this was so painful, but trust me, it cut to the core.

Jesus Understands Betrayal

There is no question that the knife of betrayal is wicked and sharp. The ugly wound it inflicts is painful and oozes with hurt and anger.

"Where are you, God? Why did this happen?" I screamed over and over as I replayed poignant scenes of our friendship in my mind. Screaming matches with God can ease the pain, but they must cease long enough to hear His voice. It took time for the acid in my stomach to stop churning and the taunting noises in my head to be still. But, I finally was able to hear Him say words that changed my life: "Dianne, don't you know that I, of all people, understand the pain of betrayal? Trust Me to handle this for you."

Of course Jesus gets betrayal! One of His closest friends, Judas, betrayed Him to the Roman authorities, who acquiesced to the peoples' horrific demands to "Crucify Him, crucify Him!" This was the ultimate betrayal by His very own people, the people Jesus loved and longed to gather as a mother hen gathers her chicks.

Jesus not only understands betrayal, He's "been there, done that." And He really does know how to handle betrayal and how to heal the destructive pain that betrayal leaves in its wake. How does Jesus do this? He gives us the choice to trust Him. It may not feel great, and our minds may be spinning with doubt, but we can choose.

Because He lives inside, with easy access to my turmoil, His help is right there. He is not a distant God that I must beg and cajole to "come down" and help me. No, He lives inside me. He is right there, waiting for me to trust Him.

Trust the One Who Knows

When Jesus said I could trust Him to handle my pain of betrayal, I made the decision to do that—trust the One in me by His Spirit. I chose to trust Him to deal with the pain I had no way to handle on my own. I wasn't tempted to fall back on one of the world's temporary (and ineffective) solutions, such as bingeing on food, drugs, alcohol, or such. I find it far better to trust Jesus. Because He lives inside, with easy access to my turmoil, His help is right there. He is not a distant God that I must beg and cajole to "come down" and help me. No, He lives inside me. He is right there, waiting for me to trust Him. And so I responded to Him:

"Yes, Jesus, You know how to handle this. You endured betrayal. I give You my pain and my confusion. I trust You to heal me as You best know how. Holy Spirit, comfort me. Keep me from bitterness, unforgiveness, and revenge."

Such a prayer brings true healing. This releases supernatural help. I knew the prayer had accomplished true healing when I saw Jane at the local Kohl's department store about six months later. I did not angrily escape to the dressing room. I did not immediately exit the store. No, I approached her with genuine peace in my heart (I did not say "love" in my heart) and was able to greet her with warmth and kindness.

In Jesus, we have peace, because He has overcome betrayal. His Spirit in us brings real help in tough times.

We Need the Spirit's Help in Tough Times

Some of you have suffered much worse betrayals in your marriages, families, or friendships than I have. In such devastating relational breakdowns, it can be tempting to think unforgiveness is an effective weapon to use against those who hurt us. But that is a lie. Unforgiveness and bitterness are weapons of our own destruction if we insist on holding onto them. Their poison kills us from the inside out. Jesus is the Master of forgiveness. This is the one gift from Him we often need in our troubled relationships. He can bring this to us in unusual ways. As always, the Holy Spirit is a great Helper.

Gary's Story of Forgiveness

Listen to my friend Gary's story:

For years I had avoided situations in the church where I would en-counter a man with whom I was very angry and who I felt had deeply offended me. I had tried to muster forgiveness, but I knew it was not genuine. The morning of November 20th, 2015, I awoke to a clear word in my head from the Holy Spirit that I should attend an upcoming church leadership retreat I was invited to, but where this man would also be. I did not want to go but reluctantly agreed.

We arrived just as the retreat was starting. Within a few minutes I realized that not only would I need to handle close social interaction with the man, but also he was a centerpiece of the meeting. Intense anger arose in me at my pastor for not telling me, and at the man for no reason other than my "justified" bitterness. I began to think about how to just sneak out. The only problem was that I knew through many confirmations that the Holy Spirit had instructed me to attend.

It was then that I choked on the hull of an almond. I started coughing and gagging and I had to leave the room to get water and cough it out. When I came in and sat back down I immediately heard very clearly in my head, "You have more than a nut stuck in your throat." Of course I understood God was referring to my unforgiveness and bitterness stuck in me toward this man. Then I again heard very clearly, "Do you love Me?" I answered quietly, "Of course." Then came, "Do you love Me more than you hate him?"

*In that moment, a flood of understanding about the power of our love for Christ started to come. I realized that as Christ has carried all past, present, and future sin, sickness, and pain, **that He has also carried any and all sin or betrayal committed against me!** I saw Christ standing there between me and the man with whom I was angry. Christ had carried this man's offense and was standing there in the man's place. My anger and hate would have to be directed at Christ; OR I could choose to LOVE CHRIST instead—for what He had done for the man.*

I never realized the unlimited power that my love of Christ has. In that moment, as I enjoyed my expression of love for Jesus, the ball of anger and hurt that I was feeling inside me vanished. The rest of the weekend was difficult for me, but the hate and bitterness lifted.

I do love Jesus and that love is far greater than any other feeling of bitterness or unforgiveness. This empowered me to let go of my unforgiveness and bitterness toward this man. Following the retreat, I met with the man to forgive and to seek forgiveness. We have since met more times in an effort to reconcile and build a healthy relationship. I am free from the "bitter nut" stuck in my throat!

Do Not Grieve the Holy Spirit

Jesus wants to help us see forgiveness through His eyes and His work, not our own. We grieve the Holy Spirit when we hold on to unforgiveness, because He knows that Jesus has paid a monster price for this gift.

> *And do not grieve the Holy Spirit of God, by whom you were sealed for the day of redemption. Let all bitterness and wrath and anger and clamor and slander be put away from you, along with all malice. Be kind to one another, tenderhearted, forgiving one another, as God in Christ forgave you (Ephesians 4:31-32 ESV).*

We can literally let go of all that ugly crud that clogs our throat and heart. We can choose to forgive. We know Jesus, who has already forgiven our enemy, has forgiven us, too.

> All tough times are met in a similar way: trust the One in us who has lived a full life on earth and has endured every temptation, trial, and tough time any human can experience.

Trust the One Inside Us

Betrayal is only one of the many tough times in our lives when we need the Holy Spirit's help. All tough times are met in a similar way: trust the One in us who has lived a full life on earth and has endured every temptation, trial, and tough time any human can experience. Trust the One in us who has forgiven all of us, all our sins.

> *Now that we know what we have—Jesus, this great High Priest with ready access to God—let's not let it slip through our fingers. We don't have a priest who is out of touch with our reality. He's been through weakness and testing, experienced it all—all but the sin. So let's walk right up to Him and get what He is so ready to give. Take the mercy, accept the help (Hebrews 4:14-16 MSG).*

He, by His Spirit, is an amazing Helper in us. He is not out of touch with our reality. Take His mercy, accept His help. Make that choice by faith, despite feelings that fluctuate. Then turn and give His mercy and help to those who hurt us the most, because Jesus took their sin, too. He loves and forgives them, too.

Do we love Him more than we hate them? Pray: "Help me, Holy Spirit. Help me to choose to forgive and love those who have hurt me."

Jesus is Our Peace

This is not just a nice platitude. This is truth. And so many of us need His peace—the peace that surpasses understanding—because tough times disrupt our lives. They throw everything into chaos. One of the most disruptive things in a parent's life is a rebellious teenage child.

When one of our four sons was 16 years old, he took a turn for the worse—a real walk on the wild side. He had been a pretty great kid up till then. He did his homework and weekly chores. He mowed yards with his brothers and played basketball with friends. He helped fix the neighbor's bike and attended church every week. Then, out of nowhere, things changed. It started with calls from the teacher alerting us that he was truant from school, and escalated to calls from the police warning us that he was vandalizing vehicles. Next came drinking parties on the local golf course and grades that plummeted to barely passing. We scolded, grounded, took car keys, limited TV, and tried a host of other desperate measures, but he only got worse, more defiant, and more determined to make our entire family miserable. Our whole household was in massive chaos and tension.

Pleading with God

I am by nature a peacekeeper, and this tendency intensified my misery. There was no peace to keep. Things were out of my control! I needed help.

I cried out to God. I pleaded with Him to show me how to pray, what demons to cast out, what types of discipline to use—anything to bring peace. Nothing had worked. But God did not offer me a silver bullet solution.

> One morning as I was again begging the Holy Spirit to help me through this tough time, He said plainly, "Jesus is your peace. You keep trying to get peace some way or some how, but Peace lives in you. You want the circumstances to change or your son to be 'fixed.' Just receive Jesus as your Peace."

One morning as I was again begging the Holy Spirit to help me through this tough time, He said plainly, "Jesus is your peace. You keep trying to get peace someway or somehow, but Peace lives in you. You want the circumstances to change or your son to be 'fixed.' Just receive Jesus as your Peace."

What? That seemed too easy, too nebulous. I did not totally understand what this meant, but I trusted the voice of the Spirit. So, I prayed: "Jesus, You are my Peace. I have tried to get peace, to make the circumstances and my son change, to do anything for peace. I trust You. I receive You as my Peace."

Change

Circumstances did not change overnight. Our son did not change overnight. But I did. And this simple revelation bled over into many different aspects as I trusted the Holy Spirit to make real to me that Jesus is my Peace. Jesus is my Faith. Jesus is my Joy. Jesus is my All and All. And Jesus lives in me by His Spirit.

That wild, rebellious son spent a few more months wreaking havoc in our family, but finally came to his senses (thank you, Holy Spirit!). My husband and I were able to hear the Spirit's directions more clearly, enforce discipline with love, and pray in faith as Peace ruled in our hearts. That "wild rebellious son" is now a 37-year-old amazing father of four who teaches rowdy high school teens. These students routinely vote him their favorite teacher. Yes, he truly knows, understands, and loves teenagers. And he, like me, loves the Holy Spirit.

Storms of Life Bring Fear

Storms in life stir fear and desperation—whether these are "bad" kids, bad debts, a bad boss, or just an all-around bad day! But Jesus questioned His disciples for not trusting Him in a fierce, life-threatening storm:

> *When Jesus woke up, He rebuked the wind and said to the waves, "Silence! Be still!" Suddenly the wind stopped, and there was a great calm. Then He asked them, "Why are you afraid? Do you still have no faith?" (Mark 4:39-40 NLT).*

Jesus is more than "in our boat" during the storm. Jesus is actually in us! No matter what the trial or trouble, we are never alone; we truly have God's gift of live-in help. Why should we be afraid? We can trust Him. Jesus is our Peace—inside of us. Jesus is the author of Faith—His faith—released in us. Storms may rage all around us, but Peace lives in us. Faith is there. Simply choose to believe Him. And, yes, the storm will be still, first in us, and then in our circumstances.

Dawn's Story

Just this week I received a note from Dawn, a friend in our church family. She had battled through a stormy time with her daughter Kate:

> *In the middle of the darkest time when I honestly wondered if Kate would survive this, God spoke to me very powerfully. As I was praying, no, begging, for God to intervene, He told me two things. The first was that I was to be silent. I was not to talk with others about the situation. I was not to talk to Kate about it. I was to simply love her and let God work. Wow, it was hard, but I obeyed.*

> *Second, He said, "I am working in this. I have called her to lead worship." I clung to that promise for years and tried to "simply" let God work. I never said anything to her, just watched as He groomed and grew*

her into the woman she is today. I guess my point is that while He was healing Kate, He was healing me. He is good!

Yes! Jesus was healing Dawn, too. She knows and has experienced that the Spirit will personally guide every person safely through the storm. We only need to listen and obey—with His help, of course! Kate is now a beautiful, happily married woman who leads worship in our Healing Rooms and has a successful counseling practice where the Spirit uses Kate's darkest years to bring hope to others. She knows that Jesus is in those who have placed their faith in Him, and Jesus will dispel all darkness.

Jesus is the Light in Our Darkness

"I struggled with depression pretty much the first 22 years of my life," said Darren, a 33-year-old father of two adorable children. "After I met Jesus, I had some relief, thanks to different inner healing prayers that helped me process my pain. However, I would only get so much help and then I was back for 'Inner Healing 2,' then 'Inner Healing 3.' After I heard the full Gospel—the Good News that *I was crucified, buried, and raised with Christ*—I suddenly had a fresh faith. I stopped trying to fix a dead, depressed me and I stopped looking in the rearview mirror of my life. I was done analyzing and blaming the past. I asked the Holy Spirit to help me live this new life where I was now hidden in Christ and He in me. The Light of the World lived in me! I trusted Him to penetrate, dispel, and deal with all my dark depression. I discovered the new me. I am one happy man!"

Darren's story is powerful and personal. There is no panacea for depression. I would never make light of the darkness of depression. It is real. It is devastating. It is deadly, and it devours both young and old. I would also never make light of helpful inner healing processes that bring some light to the darkness and hope to the hopeless. But Jesus is our Light, and He is in us. This is the truth that sets us free. Inner healing will only be helpful insofar as it leads you to that truth. Sometimes our efforts can get in the way. We end up focusing too much on the darkness and what will make it go away. We may try counseling, therapy, medication, and even more prayer. All of these can be helpful in discerning the truth, which the Spirit is eager to reveal:

The Light shines in the darkness, and the darkness can never extinguish it (John 1:5 NLT).

Jesus spoke to the people once more and said, "I am the Light of the world. If you follow Me, you won't have to walk in darkness, because you will have the Light that leads to life" (John 8:12 NLT)

We can trust Jesus to deal with our darkness. He is the Light of the world. He is the Light in us.

> It was a powerful revelation for me to discover that Jesus is actually in my darkness and not disgusted by it. He wasn't standing aloof, waiting for me to find my way through the darkness. He knew how to penetrate my darkness and was right there, doing so, as I trusted Him.

Jesus is Not Disgusted by Our Darkness

It was a powerful revelation for me to discover that Jesus is actually in my darkness and not disgusted by it. He wasn't standing aloof, waiting for me to find my way through the darkness. He knew how to penetrate my darkness and was right there, doing so, as I trusted Him. Much of my darkness had to do with my perfectionism and performance-oriented personality. I feared failure, and thought Jesus did too! The Holy Spirit led me into the truth that Jesus in me was dispelling the darkness as I let go of my fear and trusted His love for me. He spoke to me, "Dianne, you are not going to be God's first failure!" I have had to recall this truth many, many times. Thankfully, the Holy Spirit brings all things to our remembrance!

Ask Him and then allow Him to shine His light where He knows is best. Keep your eyes on Him, not on the problems. Trust His love and power. Share your heart with others who will listen to you and pray in faith for your freedom. His Light shines in our darkness, and the darkness can never extinguish it!

A Wise Approach: Two Questions

I love how author and speaker Graham Cooke teaches us to deal with adversity of any kind. In his *Brilliant Perspectives* blog entry, "Two Questions to Ask When Trials Come" (http://bit.ly/2jG5LW8), Cooke gives us two important questions to ask:

1. When we face adversity, we should first stop and ask God what the adversity means. And as we ask, Cooke says, we should remember that we live in the Kingdom, and know that God can use that adversity to strengthen our relationship with Him.

2. Then we should ask, okay, Lord, what should we do with this adversity?

Asking such open-ended questions—"What does this mean?" and "What should we do?" —frees us to hear the Spirit and access His wisdom and empowerment to handle the adversity. We don't focus on, or cower in fear of, the adversity itself; we open up to the solution and resolution of that adversity, to the outcome that God has for us—and God's outcomes are always good.

I find Cooke's advice is especially helpful for those who want to ask, *Why?*: Why did this happen? Why did God allow this? Why me? The *why* question rarely leads to healthy progress. But when we focus on the good that our good God will bring from a difficult time, we find faith stirring in our hearts in anticipation of what's ahead.

The Gift of Prayer

One year at Christmas I was burdened for various family situations. Each of our children faced different tough hurdles—a job dilemma, a child's illness, grad school disappointment, surgery, and financial struggle, to name a few. I found myself tempted to ask, "Why, God?" Before long, I was trapped in a cul-de-sac of doubt and fear. I had prayed about these and asked God for help, but I always ran out of words in just five minutes. I felt weak and powerless in my own prayers. "What does all this mean, Lord?" I asked. The Spirit had answers for me. He was ready to help:

> *And the Holy Spirit helps us in our weakness. For example, we don't know what God wants us to pray for. But the Holy Spirit prays for us with groanings that cannot be expressed in words. And the Father who knows all hearts knows what the Spirit is saying, for the Spirit pleads for us believers in harmony with God's own will (Romans 8:26-27 NLT).*

When I am weak and cannot figure out how to pray, the Spirit prays for me and through me. This may be general groanings, but most often, it is praying in a language we don't know, but God does. This is praying in tongues (the gift we learned about in Chapter 3).

I decided to give each of our five children and their families the gift of prayer—prayer in the Spirit. I promised to intentionally pray 15 minutes in the Spirit every day for each family. I sat down, closed my eyes, pictured every person, and let the Spirit pray in tongues through me. It was not difficult, but it did take daily discipline.

Praying in the Spirit Brings Good

One year later, we gathered for our annual Christmas Eve dinner and shared our highs and lows of the year. It was overwhelming to me that almost every conflict and challenge had been resolved—some in surprising ways that I would never have dreamed. I wept with joy and thankfulness. Then I heard the Holy Spirit tell me to read the passage again—but include the next verse:

> *And we know that God causes everything to work together for the good of those who love God and are called according to His purpose for them (Romans 8:28 NLT).*

What the Holy Spirit wanted me to see was Romans 8:26-27 precedes Romans 8:28. My praying in the Spirit—in complete harmony with the Father's will even when I had no idea—resulted in Him bringing "the good" promised in Romans 8:28. Yes! He had caused all things to work together for good as I had prayed in the Spirit, trusting His answers.

From that moment on, I have been even more committed to praying in the Spirit, especially in tough times. I am sure He knows how to pray through me, and God will bring good out of those prayers.

Misquoted and Misunderstood Verse

Romans 8:28 is an oft-quoted verse in the church. It is used to comfort those in tragic or tough situations, and many misinterpret the verse, believing that God actually causes those tragic or tough things and then brings good in the end. I do not agree with that theology at all. Our God is good, and He is good all the time. Satan is bad, and is bad all the time. God brings good out of Satan's bad. We can trust our good God! Wait and watch how He redeems.

Grace Abounding

Our church was (and still is!) experiencing a widespread Holy Spirit revelation of God's amazing grace. So many of us have been set free from years of condemnation and shame. It has been exhilarating to know that Jesus's finished work really finished our sinfulness and gave us new, clean hearts and His gift of righteousness. Jesus continues to get bigger, better, and more beautiful than we have ever imagined. But not all of our church family has agreed.

License to Sin?

Scott's face was red with frustration and his voice was tense with anger. "When you tell people all their sin is forgiven—past, present, and future—you are just giving them a license to sin. That is 'greasy grace' and outright heresy!" he said. "I will stop this dangerous doctrine of so-called grace. It is flat-out wrong!" Scott (not his real name) wasted no time following through on his threat, and provoked the painful departure of frightened church members.

Of course, people do not need a "license" to sin; they do very well without that! But yes, the outlandish Gospel of Grace—the Good News that Jesus actually wiped out all sin—has been stirring controversy for centuries. These same accusations were thrown at Paul, and thankfully, he recorded his response to the Romans:

> *What shall we say then? Are we to continue in sin that grace may abound? By no means! How can we who died to sin still live in it? Do you not know that all of us who have been baptized into Christ Jesus were baptized into His death? We were buried therefore with Him by baptism into death, in order that, just as Christ was raised from the dead by the glory of the Father, we too might walk in newness of life (Romans 6:1-4 ESV).*

Yes! We are dead to sin. We were buried with Christ and raised up to now walk in newness of life. We are free from sin, condemnation, guilt, and shame, and are empowered with God's grace and His Spirit to live as new creations.

Yes! We are dead to sin. We were buried with Christ and raised up to now walk in newness of life. We are free from sin, condemnation, guilt, and shame, and are empowered with God's grace and His Spirit to live as new creations. This is not a license to sin. This is freedom *from* sin!

> *There is therefore now no condemnation for those who are in Christ Jesus. For the law of the Spirit of life has set you free in Christ Jesus from the law of sin and death (Romans 8:1-2 ESV).*

This is a radical new lifestyle! No more excuses. No more blaming. We are new, and we can choose to set our minds on the Spirit.

> *For to set the mind on the flesh is death, but to set the mind on the Spirit is life and peace (Romans 8:6 ESV).*

The Spirit reminds us who we really are: righteous, clean, holy children of God, free from sin and at peace.

Temptations Do Come

Am I saying we won't ever be tempted again? No! Just yesterday I had the opportunities to fight with my husband, gossip about the neighbor, eat four cookies instead of two, and continue watching a slimy movie. Paul reminds us:

> *The temptations in your life are no different from what others experience. And God is faithful. He will not allow the temptation to be more than you can stand. When you are tempted, He will show you a way out so that you can endure (1 Corinthians 10:13 NLT).*

God is faithful—Just tune in to the God inside of you! Whether it is a big temptation (immorality, idolatry, etc.,) or little, like the ones I mentioned, God is always right there showing us a way out so we can endure and overcome.

I like to be "honest to God"—confessing to Him my struggle and talking with Him about it. (Of course, He already knows and sees, but it's important for us to confess our struggles—when we try to ignore them or hide them, that's when problems crop up.) We simply listen and obey, and depend on His love and power. The Holy Spirit reminds me who I really am—a righteous, loved daughter who has God's grace to live that way.

Jesus Helps with Each Day's Problems

The keys had been lost for five days. We had looked everywhere—in and out of the house. Now the freshly fallen snow halted the outdoor search, and we retreated to scour the couch, laundry, and even the trash—one more time. No luck! The car, on loan from a college friend, needed to be driven back to Chicago in just two more days. We needed help! Just as I was about to explode with anger at my negligent son for misplacing the only set of keys, I thought: "Why not ask the Holy Spirit?" Sure enough, soon one of us saw a picture in our mind's eye of the car's carpet with the keys lodged underneath. A quick trip to the car proved Jesus had solved the problem—thanks to the Spirit.

We really can trust Jesus with each day's problems, big and small:

And now just as you trusted Christ to save you, trust Him, too, for each day's problems; live in vital union with Him. Let your roots grow down into Him and draw up nourishment from Him. See that you go on growing in the Lord, and become strong and vigorous in the truth you were taught. Let your lives overflow with joy and thanksgiving for all He has done (Colossians 2:6-7 TLB).

> We trusted Jesus to save us, and we can trust Him for each day's problems. He really does care about the nitty-gritty of our lives…. As we let our roots go down into Him through unforced rhythms of grace and make the daily choices to trust His love, we are nourished and become strong and vigorous in the truth.

We trusted Jesus to save us, and we can trust Him for each day's problems. He really does care about the nitty-gritty of our lives. We live in vital union with Him. He loves us. As we let our roots go down into Him through unforced rhythms of grace and make the daily choices to trust His love, we are nourished and become strong and vigorous in the truth. Then our lives truly do overflow with joy and thanksgiving—even in the middle of tough times.

Together in Tough Times

All of life is best done in community with one another—family, church, small groups; but it is especially helpful when we go through tough times. The Spirit in each of us touches one another. Contrary to what the enemy wants you to believe in tough times, we are *never* alone—even if it is "just" us and the Holy Spirit.

We love you, Holy Spirit! Thank You for helping us trust You in tough times. Thank You for reminding us of Your presence and power within us. Thank You for bringing good out of the trials, temptations, and even the tragedies we face.

REFLECT *on the SPIRIT'S WORK in YOUR LIFE*

- What has been your first reaction when you encounter tough times?

- What have you thought was God's role in tough times?

- What has been the most difficult thing you have endured (tragedy, betrayal, abuse, etc.)? Share your experience.

- What has helped you the most in tough times?

RESPOND *to the SPIRIT'S WORK IN YOUR LIFE*

- How might you handle tough times differently now—with the Spirit's help?

- Have you tried praying in the Spirit in a tough time? If so, share. If not, would you be willing to try this week?

- How has the Spirit used other people to help you through tough times?

RELATE *to the SPIRIT'S WORK in OTHER'S LIVES*

- Watch Ashton and Jon share their story on the accompanying DVD of trusting the Holy Spirit during a tough time in their marriage.

- Discuss your responses with the small group.

Chapter Six:
Help! How Do I Pray
for Others, Holy Spirit?

The Holy Spirit is eager for us to share God's love and power.
This is such an amazing privilege we have right now:
be Jesus's Body on earth. We get to speak His words and
do His works. The Holy Spirit wants to give gifts to each of
us to do even greater works than Jesus, especially outside
the church walls, in a very "naturally supernatural" way.

"Lay down your life for others. Love your enemies. Announce the King-dom has come. Heal the sick. Raise the dead. Say 'no' to self. Pray for those who persecute you. Cast out demons. Go into all the world. Do greater works than I. Freely give as you have freely received."

Yikes! Who can do any of this? And yet, these are just a few of the in-structions Jesus gave to us, His disciples. These are for *all* disciples, not just trained ministers or church employees. We are all sent by Jesus to continue His work here on earth. And there is a lot of work to be done: cancers still kill, PTSD is widespread, Parkinson's and Alzheimer's have no cures, and more and more families struggle with autism. And of course, many people do not yet know Jesus and His unfailing love.

Everybody Gets to Play

We are Jesus's Body, and we are sent to speak His words and do His works. We are not our own. We have been bought with a price. This is a privilege. And it can be so much fun, too! John Wimber, founder of the Vineyard Movement, coined the phrase "Everybody gets to play." No seminary degree required. No ordination needed. Just a willing heart and a tenacious spirit.

Men and women through the centuries have tried, failed, and tried again, somewhat succeeded, tried harder, and failed again—to do all that Jesus commanded. These commands are no small potatoes. As a matter of fact, this life is downright impossible. And that is exactly what the Holy Spirit cannot wait for us to discover and admit. He is waiting for us to cry "Help!" He is ready to reveal the secret.

The Secret

It was the mid '80s, and our small church had experienced a growth spurt, accompanied by ravenous appetites in all of us. We wanted to be and do all that Jesus commanded. We were hungry for more! At the suggestion of a local professor at the University of Illinois, we invited a woman teacher from Atlanta, Georgia, to come share what the Spirit was showing her.

"There is a secret to the Christian life," this elegant Southern woman drawled to her eager listeners. "And this secret will change your whole life. But before I tell you the secret, I want y'all to write down what you think this secret is."

Each of us quickly scribbled a variety of responses: fervent prayer, frequent fasting, extreme sacrifice, sin-free lifestyle, daily witnessing, and memorizing the Bible were just a few things written. Then we took turns sharing our answers to the teacher's question: "What is the secret to the Christian life?" With each response, the woman shook her head and softly said, "No, that is a great thing to do, but that is not the secret to the Christian life."

What could the secret possibly be? Finally, she told us all to turn in our Bibles to Colossians 1 and read what Paul said was the secret:

> *For God wanted them to know that the riches and glory of Christ are for you Gentiles, too. And this is the secret:* **CHRIST LIVES IN YOU.** *This gives you assurance of sharing His glory (Colossians 1:27 NLT).*

Christ lives in you. Exactly! Jesus never intended for us to do what He told us to do apart from a dynamic, vital union with Him. We were never supposed to try to live the "Christian life." Instead, God's invitation to us has always been to join Him in living the "Christ life." And to make sure we could share the glory of that life, He designated us as His home and moved in.

Christ in You

Christ in you is the secret not just to the Christian life, but to all of life. That is why we are sent to live this new life "in His Name," and this includes praying for others who need His help. "In His Name" is not just some little phrase we attach to every prayer we say. We know the secret to the Christian life is our union with Him. We have learned much about this union with God in the previous chapters, and we will continue to grow in the reality of this.

All Jesus asks us to do, we do in His Name, in union with Him, and the Holy Spirit helps us all along the way. This is the same Spirit who lived in Jesus. We are not left to ourselves or to some second-rate power source. We have *the* Holy Spirit in us. He is the One who has power over sin, sickness, and yes, even death.

The Same Spirit

The same Spirit that raised Jesus from the dead now lives in you and in me:

> *The Spirit of God, who raised Jesus from the dead, lives in you (Romans 8:11a NLT).*

This is one powerful Spirit! He lives in us, and He has many powerful gifts to share with us to help us care for others. We ask: "How do you help us pray for others, Holy Spirit?"

He first wants to help us see people the way He does. It is difficult to truly pray and care for others when we are blinded to a person's worth and value. But, in union with Jesus, we can see that value!

Do Not Judge

I did not consider myself a judgmental person. I am a trained special education teacher, equipped to work with handicapped children, who often suffer the judgments of others. I witnessed firsthand the damage done by cruel judgments, uttered in careless jest by children and adults alike. In addition, as a teacher, I tried to be extra sensitive to the cultural and ethnic differences among my students. I never preferred one child to another. Even after I stopped teaching, I carried these values and beliefs with me. I proudly lived Jesus's words: "Do not judge." Hence, it was a strong jolt to my pride when, one day, the Holy Spirit unequivocally exposed to me just how judgmental (and icky) I really was.

Which Neighbors to Invite

My husband and I wanted to obey Jesus's command to share the Good News with our neighbors. We decided to invite people to our home for a cookout, but as we planned the party, we systematically eliminated people from the guest list.

"Oh, he's a science professor at the university... too intellectual and anti-God. Oh, she is a divorcee... too damaged. Oh, they are from the Middle East... Muslim, no doubt." And so it went until our guest list was reduced to a few white, middle-class families with small children—just like us! Something was wrong with this picture.

All Made in His Image

We were not only unjustly judging these folks, but we had also lost the true Good News—Jesus loves *everybody*. Jesus died for *everybody*. Jesus sees *everybody* as valuable, made in His image, and most welcome in His family. And no one's acceptance has anything to do with ethnicity, intellect, or lifestyle—good or bad. God loves every human being, made in His image, of much worth and value, and He wanted (and needed) me to see this. If I was ever going to be a true reflection of Jesus to my neighbors and be trusted to pray for them in Jesus's Name, I needed to see them as Jesus sees them. I needed to take off my judge's robe.

Take off the Judge's Robe

So I took off that robe and asked Jesus to help me see people—all people—as He sees them. This is foundational to the Holy Spirit flowing through us as we pray in Jesus's Name for others. Oh, sure, I still mess this up all the time. I walk in the airport and size people up: tall, fat, sloppy, rich, noisy, pretty, old... you name it. I judge those around me, instead of seeing them with Jesus's eyes and loving them with His heart. At times like that, the Holy Spirit whispers, "Take off the judge's robe, Di." And before you know it, I am engaged in a conversation with a frazzled nurse who missed her airline connection and is stranded for the night. With genuine compassion in my heart and eyes that see beyond her messy appearance, I ask: "Can I pray for you right now?" She agrees with tears streaming down her face. The Holy Spirit helps me pray in Jesus's name and with Jesus's love.

Can I Pray for You Right Now?

These are just seven simple words that anyone can ask—anywhere, anytime. What an awesome privilege we have to offer prayer to those around us who need help. This is not just for trained ministers or full-time church employees. This is for all of us. Jesus sends all of us to be salt and light wherever we go. This is why we are here! Jesus said:

> *Let me tell you why you are here. You're here to be salt-seasoning that brings out the God-flavors of this earth.... Here's another way to put it: You're here to be light, bringing out the God-colors in the world. God is not a secret to be kept... Now that I've put you there on a hilltop, on a light stand—shine! Keep open house; be generous with your lives. By opening up to others, you'll prompt people to open up with God, this generous Father in heaven (Matthew 5:13-16 MSG).*

The metaphor "salt and light" can be a bit confusing, but I think this translation helps bring clarity. When we see others as people made in God's image, having "God-flavors and God-colors," so to speak, we are ready to open up to them without judging them. All people are made in God's image, whether we can see it or not. All people have God's color and God's flavor in their lives, whether they know it or not. If we do know that about them, then we genuinely treat them as valued. They, in turn, open up to us and to the God in us. Sometimes we just listen. Other times, we can offer, "Can I pray for you right now?"

Most People Say "Yes"

My husband and I were on our evening walk when we crossed paths with our neighbor, Ruth. Right away we could tell she was dejected, so we stopped to ask how things were going. After she disclosed some difficulties at home, we asked if we could pray for her. "Yes," she sighed, and we said a simple 15-second prayer there on the sidewalk as the sun set behind us. Whether we are acquainted with a person or not, we almost never have someone reject this offer of prayer.

Right Now?

However, most people are surprised that we mean we will pray right at that moment, not later when we get home. Many have never had anyone offer to pray for them in person, even those who are regular church attenders. Most people welcome this out-of-the-ordinary, yet simple, tender touch. It is very natural and, at the same time, very supernatural. We like to say it is "naturally supernatural" and not at all "repulsively religious." Some folks have witnessed TV evangelists or church preachers pray for others in "Jeeeeez-us" name, with grandiose gestures and hyped inflection. It is a pleasant surprise to them when we act normal and ask with calm compassion, "Can I pray for you right now?"

> The great thing about this simple offer of prayer is that we can do this almost anywhere—in the Wal-Mart checkout line when the clerk says she has a bad headache or in the bleachers when the mom next to us is concerned about her injured daughter.

We Can Pray Anywhere

The great thing about this simple offer of prayer is that we can do this almost anywhere—in the Wal-Mart checkout line when the clerk says she has a bad headache or in the bleachers when the mom next to us is concerned about her injured daughter. My friends Dave and Judy rarely eat at a restaurant without offering prayer to a hassled waitress or a busy busboy. They have partnered with the Holy Spirit over and over in this way wherever they go to eat and have seen many people open up to God.

Best Ways to Partner with God

Others in our church family, The Vineyard Church of Central Illinois, have discovered the best ways for them to partner with the Holy Spirit. Each person is different and has a unique sphere of influence. It takes some trial and error to discover your best ways to partner with God.

Burnsey has many great conversations on her train rides to Chicago. Heather notes who needs encouragement at the spa. Toni prays for those who come to the food pantry. Jamie's Uber customers are often blessed with prayer, and Charles stays alert in his apartment building for those in need.

We do not have to know a special script or carry our Bible. On the contrary, we carry Christ in us, and His love flows out of us. He shows us what He is doing in our day, along the way, to help the people He loves through us.

The Father Showed Jesus What He was Doing

The Father is always working, and He loves to show us what He is doing. This is exactly how Jesus ministered so powerfully. John tells us:

So Jesus said to them, "Truly, truly, I say to you, the Son can do nothing of His own accord, but only what He sees the Father doing. For whatever the Father does, that the Son does likewise. For the Father loves the Son and shows Him all that He Himself is doing..." (John 5:19-20 ESV).

It seems crazy (but is actually encouraging!) that Jesus could no nothing on His own. Jesus did only what the Father showed Him to do, and He was very aware that He could only do that. The Father loved to show Jesus what He was up to. Jesus just had to be alert, see what the Father was doing, and be obedient. It is the same for us.

Some of you might say, "Yes, but Jesus had an advantage—He was, after all, the Son of God. So of course He had this special intimacy with the Father." Well, the reality is that Jesus has given us this very same advantage—we are all sons and daughters of the Father! And we have the Holy Spirit in us. What could be more intimate than that? So we, too, can tune in to what the Father is doing, through the help of the Holy Spirit—and when we tune in, we can't help but be excited to be part of what the Father is doing in our lives at this very moment, wherever we are. We see wonderful possibilities open up to us as, through the Holy Spirit, we see what the Father is doing *right now,* and how He invites us to be a part of it. That is an open invitation He extends to us 24/7/365.

We Don't Pray for Everyone

If only we were as wise as Jesus! Some, when they learn they can pray this way for others, think they "have" to pray for everyone. Others may try to do this in their own strength. No, we can only do what the Father shows us and only in union with the Spirit. It would be one long trip to the grocery store if we stopped to pray for everyone we saw. It would be a surefire route to job loss if we neglected our work to pray for our officemates all day long. God does not expect us to pray for everyone we see in a day. But He does want us to see what He is up to.

Learn to See What God is Doing

It is so critical to learn how to see what God is doing. The cool thing is that He is always working, so we do not have to manufacture opportunities. We do not have to try to "make something happen." When I first learned to pray for strangers, I made a ton of mistakes. I thought God expected me to always pray for the person sitting next to me on the airplane. I remember a tired soldier and a busy executive who were not too happy about my attempts at conversation. Frankly, I was relieved to return to my *People* magazine and not engage with real people! However, my friend Robby Dawkins frequently has powerful encounters on airplanes as God shows him what He is doing. His stories encourage me, but I do not try to be Robby. I try instead to see what God is doing, and then be me. Each of us is different, and God knows that.

> When the Holy Spirit does nudge us to stop and offer conversation or prayer, we can and do. This usually comes as a gentle "knowing" inside as we feel God's love rise in us. We realize God planned this encounter in the grocery store or at the gym. We stop and listen to the Spirit.

Be Alert

We do have to be alert. We do have to look people in the eye and not rush past and fail to acknowledge them with nary a smile. We do have to make time in our schedules so we aren't always rushing from one task to the next without any time to stop for God. When the Holy Spirit does nudge us to stop and offer conversation or prayer, we can and do. This usually comes as a gentle "knowing" inside as we feel God's love rise in us. We realize God planned this encounter in the grocery store or at the gym. We stop and listen to the Spirit.

GodStops

I like to call these GodStops. We stop to partner with God. What a privilege! Can these interrupt your day? Absolutely! Are these easy and convenient? No, not always. But, GodStops bring true joy to us and to Jesus. We leave the results up to Him. Our part is to see people as He sees them, let the Holy Spirit fill us with His compassion, and sometimes ask that simple seven-word question: "Can I pray for you right now?" This is so natural, and yet supernatural, too. There are many people who need to know and experience the love of Jesus. But there are so few who are actually willing to help with the "harvest." Matthew tells us:

> When He (Jesus) saw the crowds, He had compassion for them, because they were harassed and helpless, like sheep without a shepherd. Then He said to His disciples, "The harvest is plentiful, but the laborers are few..." (Matthew 9:35-37 ESV).

Christ lives in us. He is the secret to the Christian life. He wants to flood us with the ability to see people as He sees them—made in His image, of much worth and value. He wants to flood us with His compassion for them, because He knows they are harassed and helpless. We have Help living within us. We can give away in Jesus's Name. However, we, too, can feel helpless when it comes to praying for others. We can feel overwhelmed by "the plentiful harassed harvest" of people all around us. It can be intimidating!

No Confidence

"I was always afraid to pray for people or talk with them about Jesus," lamented Leah, a successful graduate student at the University of Illinois. "I felt helpless and powerless. I could sympathize with my friends as they shared struggles with school or relationships or even their health, but I had no faith or confidence to offer more than a weak 'I'll pray' or a halfhearted 'God will help.' Then, I met the Holy Spirit. I had no idea the Holy Spirit had a whole boatload of gifts to help me share! This changed everything."

> These spiritual gifts are for us to give away to others when we pray for them. We are just like a postman, delivering whatever the Spirit gives us for a particular person at a particular place.

The Holy Spirit Gives Gifts

The Holy Spirit does have lots of gifts to share, and they make all the difference. As we learned in Chapter 3, there is a baptism in the Spirit that is essential for empowering us to be Jesus's witnesses. Jesus is the One who told us how important the Spirit baptism is. With that Spirit immersion comes the opportunity to exercise the spiritual gifts. These spiritual gifts are for us to give away to others when we pray for them. We are just like a postman, delivering whatever the Spirit gives us for a particular person at a particular place. The spiritual gifts are given so we can help one another. Paul describes these gifts:

There are different kinds of spiritual gifts, but the same Spirit is the source of them all. There are different kinds of service, but we serve the same Lord. God works in different ways, but it is the same God who does the work in all of us.

A spiritual gift is given to each of us so we can help each other. To one person the Spirit gives the ability to give wise advice; to another the same Spirit gives a message of special knowledge. The same Spirit gives great faith to another, and to someone else the one Spirit gives the gift of healing.

He gives one person the power to perform miracles, and another the ability to prophesy. He gives someone else the ability to discern whether a message is from the Spirit of God or from another spirit.

Still another person is given the ability to speak in unknown languages, while another is given the ability to interpret what is being said. It is the one and only Spirit who distributes all these gifts. He alone decides which gift each person should have (1 Corinthians 12:4-11 NLT).

This list can seem intimidating and confusing: healing, miracles, prophecy, faith, special knowledge—yikes! The key phrase is: *it is God who does the work in all of us.* Yes, the Spirit, our live-in help, distributes gifts to each of us as needed for a specific situation. These are all supernatural gifts from

God. These are not natural talents we might possess—like speaking well, medical expertise, or extroverted confidence. No, these are God's gifts given to us to give away.

All the Gifts for All People

Early in my life as a believer, I thought each of us only received one gift and that was that. Maybe my gift was healing or prophecy or miracles. It was "my" gift and I shared it when needed, but that was all I had to give. Then I discovered that *all* of us could have *all* the gifts.

However, the Spirit decides which gift we need in any given situation. Then, that is the gift we receive from Him to give away to the hurting person at that moment. With practice, we learn how to give away the right gift at the right time to the right person. Usually, we offer to pray for someone first—we take the risk—and then we have an awareness of what the Spirit is doing and what gift or gifts He is giving.

We Pray, God Works

As we lay hands on the person, the powerful gifts of the Spirit flow through us in Jesus's name. It might be a gift of healing, as evidenced by heat or physical sensation on the person's body. It might be a word of prophecy that pops in our heads, and we speak encouragement. We may see a picture in our mind's eye of something and ask the person if it means anything. All the while, we are watching to observe how the Spirit is touching the person. Yes, we are "working," but God in us does the real work! Apart from Him we can do nothing. However....

What if Nothing Happens?

Good question, and one that I am frequently asked. This is a very real fear, and it fools us into thinking it is up to us to make sure a person is healed or miraculously touched. No! It is up to God. We are not responsible for the results—God is. Remember, apart from Him we can do nothing. And He is fine with handling the results, even when we think "nothing happened." The least that happened is that the person experienced God's love, and love is the greatest of all.

Fear of Failure

But I understand this fear. As I mentioned, I can be a perfectionistic, performance-oriented person—when left to myself (forgetting Jesus lives in me). Hence, it is a no-brainer that I can fear failure, and a real no-brainer that this fear stifles my willingness to risk praying for others. Freedom from fear of failure comes when I remember a very important truth I was taught by John Wimber, founder of the Vineyard Movement: "It's OK to fail!" Really. We do not flunk if we fail. John himself learned this the hard way; he prayed for more than 200 people over the course of many months before seeing anyone healed!!

> Will we fail? Yes, in the sense we do not always see actual healing or change. Will we make mistakes? Yep! Lots of them. We are learning, and that, as any good teacher knows, means mistakes are made. It keeps us humble, dependent on Jesus, and aware: **God does the work in all of us.**

Father's Delight

The Father is better than any earthly father, and He is not bothered by our failure. He is delighted that we took a risk, stepped out in love to pray for someone, and trusted Him for the results. Will we fail? Yes, in the sense we do not always see actual healing or change. Will we make mistakes? Yep! Lots of them. We are learning, and that, as any good teacher knows, means mistakes are made. It keeps us humble, dependent on Jesus, and aware: *God does the work in all of us.* And, by the way, the Father Himself does not call any of this "failure." He calls it faith!

Gift of Healing

Cory was enjoying the warm spring day when he saw a woman sitting on a park bench, rubbing her knee. He stopped by, introduced himself, and inquired about her knee. She said she was in pain from a torn meniscus, and the steroids had worn off. He asked if he could pray and she agreed. After several minutes, she smiled with relief and announced that the pain was gone. Wow! The Holy Spirit had released a gift of healing through Cory's prayer. Does this always happen when he prays? No! But he leaves the results up to God. "If I focus on my success or failure, I get discouraged real fast," Cory shared. "My job is to pray. God does the healing." And this is exactly how it plays out in our lives. Everybody gets to play—or as I like to say, "Everybody gets to pray!" And our prayer is not always restricted to praying for healing; sometimes we are prompted to give away the gift of prophetic encouragement.

Gift of Prophecy

A middle-aged man in a wheelchair recently shared with me that some college kids approached him at the Wal-Mart. They asked if they could pray and while he did not get healed, he told me that their words of encouragement prompted him to ask where they went to church. Bingo! The Holy Spirit was helping this man and his wife find a church home. They have been attending our church ever since. These words of encouragement—one expression of the gift of prophecy—mean we speak what God puts on our hearts for another person. As we tune in to the Spirit, we get a sense of something to say. We share it in a natural, low-key, conversational manner, and not a loud shout of: "Thus saith the Lord!"

The Miracle Question

Standing in line at the local Chipotle, Randy noticed two college guys come through the door, and he sensed the Spirit wanted him to ask them "The Miracle Question." As soon as they were seated and eating their burrito bowls, Randy struck up a casual conversation. They bantered back and forth about the latest Illini football victory, their own fraternity exploits, and their need to stop goofing off and start studying for finals. As the conversation grew more serious, Randy knew the time was right to ask the Miracle Question.

The Miracle Question is actually three questions, starting with: "May I ask you a question?" Most people respond "yes." The second question is: "If God could do one miracle for you right now, what would that be?" It can be difficult at first for people to answer this question. They want to say something like: "My grandma is sick," or "My dad needs a job," deflecting attention from themselves. But, the question is: "What miracle do YOU need from God?" So, you can rephrase this to say, "What is one prayer for yourself that you would like answered today?" After they respond, you say a simple prayer for their specific request. Then, you ask: "What do you think is the greatest miracle God could ever do for you?" After they have thought of an answer, or can't think of one, share with them the greatest miracle God could ever do for them personally: "Actually, He's already done it, and it's in the form of a gift, a very precious and costly gift. The gift of God for you is eternal life." The conversation can continue from there, depending on the interaction and responses.

Randy ended up partnering with the Holy Spirit as the two college guys received prayer for physical injuries *and* God's gift of eternal life—right there in Chipotle. Because Randy listened and spoke with genuine interest and care, the young men were receptive and not put off by "evangelistic" pressure.

Mark Marx

We are deeply indebted to our dear friend, Mark Marx from Coleraine, Ireland, who wrote, piloted, and now teaches "The Miracle Question" all over the world. Mark also has a passion for healing, and is the author of the bestselling book *Stepping Into the Impossible,* where he shares his own story of praying for the sick and launching the now world-renowned H.O.T.S.—Healing on the Streets. Grab a copy of this fabulous, inspiring book, and invite the Holy Spirit to give you new eyes to see and fresh motivation to share God's love and power.

Overwhelming!

All of this can feel somewhat overwhelming. And it is—without training and a team to help. That is why we recommend enrolling in a course at your local church where you can learn the basics of praying for others in the power of the Spirit. There are also great resources listed in our Resource section. Being part of a faith community that equips and encourages you to pray this way is the best environment for growth.

School of Kingdom Ministry

For those who want to really grow, The Vineyard Church of Central Illinois offers the School of Kingdom Ministry. This is a nine-month course that any church or group may enroll in and receive intensive instruction and practice in doing Kingdom Ministry: healing the sick, casting out demons, sharing the Gospel, and exercising all the gifts of the Spirit. Thousands of men and women around the US and the world have been trained through SoKM. See their website at http://schoolofkingdomministry.org/ for more info.

Greater Works

I circle back around to where we started this chapter—doing impossible things with Jesus. Jesus Himself said:

> *Truly, truly, I say to you, whoever believes in Me will also do the works that I do; and greater works than these will he do, because I am going to the Father (John 14:12 ESV).*

Truly, truly, this is one tough assignment: do greater works than Jesus! The only condition is "whoever believes in Me." Those who believe will do these works, because Jesus is going to the Father. Most of us would say, "I believe in Jesus." Why are we not doing greater works? I think it is important to read this verse in context with the preceding verse. Jesus addresses what this "belief in Him" entails:

> *Do you not believe that I am in the Father and the Father is in Me? The words that I say to you I do not speak on My own authority, but the Father who dwells in Me does His works. Believe Me that I am in the Father and the Father is in Me, or else believe on account of the works themselves (John 14:10-11 ESV).*

Ah, yes. There is that union again—that oneness—Jesus is in the Father and the Father is in Him and He is doing the works. Jesus wants us to believe this, *because this is the same union we have with God.* Jesus is returning to the Father—after His resurrection—and now we can know and live in this union with God the Father, just like Jesus!

> *In that day, you will know, said Jesus, I am in the Father, the Father is in Me and I am in you (John 14:20 ESV).*

This is the same union by which we will live the life as God's sons and daughters here on earth and forever, too. This is the union that gives us the power and ability to do the same and greater works. We simply ask in Jesus's Name—in union with Him—and He will do it.

Union with God

This is the same union we have been exploring throughout this book. Christ in us—the secret to the Christian life. The Holy Spirit—God's gift of live-in help. This is the same union by which we will live the life as God's sons and daughters here on earth and forever, too. This is the union that gives us the power and ability to do the same and greater works. We simply ask in Jesus's Name—in union with Him—and He will do it.

> *Whatever you ask in My Name, this I will do, that the Father may be glorified in the Son. If you ask Me anything in My Name, I will do it (John 14:10-14 ESV).*

Do I understand this? No, but I believe. I believe Jesus is in me and I am in Jesus, and His prayer to the Father is being realized right now at this time in history. Jesus prayed:

> *The glory that you have given Me I have given to them, that they may be one even as We are one, I in them and You in Me, that they may become perfectly one, so that the world may know that You sent Me and loved them even as You loved Me (John 17:22-23 ESV).*

I join with this prayer—that all of us may know the union we have with God—Father, Son, and Holy Spirit. Then the world may know that Jesus was sent by the Father to make it possible for all of us to live as He lives, in union with the Father and Spirit, and know that we are loved by the Father, even as He is loved.

Many Bible teachers say Jesus's prayer here is about unity among denominations, races, and individuals with differences. While Jesus does want us to all get along, that is not the meaning of His prayer for oneness. He paid a huge price so we could be welcomed into the same relational union as the Trinity. When we grasp the reality of this union and live it out, the world will know the love of Jesus as we speak His words and do His works. This is mind-blowing to me! This is not what is normally taught as typical Christianity. This is the mystery hidden from ages past:

> *The mystery hidden for ages and generations but now revealed to his saints. To them God chose to make known how great among the Gentiles are the riches of the glory of this mystery, which is Christ in you, the hope of glory (Colossians 1:26-27 ESV).*

This is the secret to the Christian life: Christ in you, Christ in me. We are the home of God. Hello, Holy Spirit. Fill us with the fullness of God!

Thank You, Holy Spirit, for opening our eyes and our heart. Keep teaching us how to live in this union and give away the life, love, and power in us, in Jesus's Name! Thank You for giving us Your gifts. We want to partner with You in doing the same and greater works.

REFLECT *on the SPIRIT'S WORK in YOUR LIFE*

- What have you thought was the secret to the Christian life?

- Share how you may have struggled with judging others and why this is damaging to your ability to care for them.

- What are your thoughts about "Can I pray for you right now?"

- Have you ever prayed for another person right there and then? Share your experience.

RESPOND *to the SPIRIT'S WORK in YOUR LIFE*

- What gifts of the Spirit do you want to give away and why?

- Look for GodStops this week and stop to cooperate with the Spirit.

- Pray Jesus's prayer from John 17 this week. Be more aware of the union you have with God. This is the secret to the Christian life.

RELATE *to the SPIRIT'S WORK in OTHER'S LIVES*

- Watch Burnsey share her story of partnering with the Holy Spirit on the accompanying DVD.

- Discuss your responses with the small group.

RESOURCES
Books, Prayers, and Other Goodies

Books

I love books, and I have grown so much from reading a wide variety. Do I agree with everything I read in those listed here? No! But that is why we "read in the Spirit," and He helps us discern truth! Invite the Holy Spirit to read along with you and teach you the deeper things of God. He is really good at this.

Chapter One

Mystical Union by John Crowder

Powerful revelation of our union with God. Get prepared to be rocked!

The Gospel in Ten Words by Paul Ellis

Best explanation of the tremendous Good News! Eye-opening, heart-changing!

Chapter Two

From Spiritual Slavery to Sonship by Jack Frost

Be free from Orphan Thinking as you read this classic!

The Great Dance by C. Baxter Kruger

God is eager to have us join His exhilarating dance and experience true joy in all. So long, dualism!

The Mirror Bible by Francois du Toit

A selection of key New Testament texts paraphrased from the Greek and intended to blow your mind!

Chapter Three

The Baptism of the Holy Spirit by Randy Clark

Easy-to-understand theology and practice from one who knows!

The Indwelling Life of Christ by Major W. Ian Thomas

Fantastic devotional to renew your mind every day: Christ lives in me!

Chapter Four

The Good and Beautiful God by James Bryan Smith

Great chapters on God's goodness and practical application through spiritual practices.

Sacred Rhythms by Ruth Haley Barton

Best book on the "unforced rhythms of grace"!

Chapter Five

Practicing His Presence by Brother Lawrence and Frank Laubach

Classic book with extra insights from a contemporary perspective.

The Shack by William Paul Young

Bestselling novel that unveils the Father, Son, and Spirit like you have never seen!

Chapter Six

Stepping Into the Impossible by Mark Marx

Be encouraged that God wants to equip you to do the impossible!

Translating God by Shawn Bolz

Fantastic instructions on how to speak prophetic encouragement and hope to all.

Five Step Prayer Model by Vineyard Resources

Great booklet for learning to pray for others with a simple model.

Prayers

Prayer is simply talking with God. He hears us and is ready to answer! Be sure to set aside time to talk with God everyday and continue listening to Him all day.

Prayer to Receive Jesus as Savior and Be Born Anew

Jesus, I want to receive You as my Savior, my Lord. I turn from my old thoughts and behaviors and ask You to take over my life and make me new. I believe You died for my sins, were buried, and rose again. Thank You that all my sins are forgiven and gone! Thank you that I actually died with You and am now new. Thank You that I am given a new heart and new life, now and forever. I want to know You, Jesus! I love You, Jesus.

Here are helpful Bible texts:

But to all who did receive Him, who believed in His name, He gave the right to become children of God, who were born, not of blood nor of the will of the flesh nor of the will of man, but of God (John 1:12-13 ESV).

And I will give you a new heart, and a new spirit I will put within you. And I will remove the heart of stone from your flesh and give you a heart of flesh. And I will put my Spirit within you, and cause you to walk in My statutes and be careful to obey My rules (Ezekiel 36:26-27 ESV).

If you confess with your mouth that Jesus is Lord and believe in your heart that God raised him from the dead, you will be saved. For with the heart one believes and is justified, and with the mouth one confesses and is saved. For the Scripture says, "Everyone who believes in Him will not be put to shame" (Romans 10:9-11 ESV).

Prayer for Baptism of the Holy Spirit

Jesus, I thank You for Your Holy Spirit. I want to overflow with Your Spirit. I want to be baptized in the Spirit. Please fill me and empower me to live and minister like You. Please fill me with all of Your gifts. I receive You and Your wonderful gifts in Jesus's Name.

Here are helpful Bible texts:

"Did you receive the Holy Spirit when you believed?" he asked them. "No," they replied, "We haven't even heard that there is a Holy Spirit."... Then when Paul laid his hands on them, the Holy Spirit came on them, and they spoke in other tongues and prophesied (Acts 19:2,6 NLT).

For John baptized with water, but you will be baptized with the Holy Spirit not many days from now.... But you will receive power when the Holy Spirit has come upon you, and you will be my witnesses in Jerusalem and in all Judea and Samaria, and to the end of the earth (Acts 1:5-8 NLT).

So if you sinful people know how to give good gifts to your children, how much more will your heavenly Father give the Holy Spirit to those who ask him (Luke 11:13 NLT).

Daily Prayers for Help!

Hello, Holy Spirit! I welcome You to help me with all of life today. Thank You for the grace to live in today. Thank You for help in living in the present in Your presence.

Jesus, are You IN me? Thank You for allowing me to know this afresh for today.

Father, I ask according to the riches of Your glory that You may grant me to be strengthened with power through Your Spirit in my inner being, so that Christ may dwell in my heart through faith—that I, being rooted and grounded in love, may have strength to comprehend with all the saints what is the breadth and length and height and depth, and to know the love of Christ that surpasses knowledge, that I may be filled with all the fullness of God (adapted from Ephesians 3:16-19 ESV).

Other Goodies

As a former teacher, I know people learn in different ways. Watching a DVD or listening to a podcast may be easier for you. Here are some helpful resources!

Hello, Holy Spirit DVD/Leader's Guide

This is a set of six individual teachings, along with inspiring stories of people whose lives have been radically changed by the Holy Spirit! These six weeks coordinate with the six chapters in this book. Great resource for small group gatherings, complete with a helpful Leader's Guide filled with questions and activations. Proven successful for life transformation. Published by The Vineyard Church of Central Illinois (**http://www.vineyardlive.us/**).

Hello, Holy Spirit Message Series

A set of six podcasts that coordinate with the six chapters of this book. Preaching outlines are included from the five different speakers. Published by The Vineyard Church of Central Illinois (**http://www.vineyardlive.us/**).

School of Kingdom Ministry

A nine-month, three-hour per week intensive training in Holy Spirit power ministry, grounded in our new identities as sons and daughters.

See website for more info: **http://schoolofkingdomministry.org/**.

My website and Facebook page

Go to my website (**http://www.dianneleman.com/**) to find teachings, book reviews, and other tidbits to help you grow. Also, connect with me on **https://www.facebook.com/dianneleman1/**.

Acknowledgments

Holy Spirit, thank You for helping me write this book! You truly are the Helper in all of life, and I love You. I never dreamed what a difference You would make in my life. Thank You for moving inside of me and refreshing me daily with Your River of Life. It is a real privilege to partner with You.

Special thanks to our Vineyard Church tribe who collaborated on the sermon series, *Hello, Holy Spirit,* that launched this book. Our communications team of Carolyn Yoder, Derek Manson, Laura Bice, Ashton Harwood, and Dusten Jenkins were fantastic and creative in producing graphics, content, and DVD footage. Our preaching team of Putty Putman, Clay Harrington, Happy Leman, and Julie Yoder shared powerful messages that track with this book's contents and add even more insight to our wonderful Helper, the Holy Spirit. It was so much fun to watch the Holy Spirit speak and move through each of you.

Thanks, too, to Katie Goulet who designed the cover and encouraged me to forge ahead when I was tempted to be discouraged, and to Tom Hanlon, who is the world's best editor, even when I gave him just a few days to do the job. And I love the creative work of Jody Boles who designed the interior for me and is so much fun to work with! Thank you!

Finally, I want to acknowledge my wonderful brother Tim Hoerr and his wife Toni, who allowed me the generous use of their condo on beautiful Coronado Island, California. That makes writing so much easier. The Holy Spirit seems to really love the beach! Thank you!

And, of course, I must acknowledge and thank my life partner of 45 years, my husband, Hap. He believes in me even when I have serious doubts, and he never (I mean never!) stops supporting and pushing me (gently!) forward. I love you, Silver Fox.

With much gratitude and love,
Di

Made in United States
Orlando, FL
03 March 2023

30636189R00085